THE PRESSURE
OF
OUR COMMON CALLING

W. A. VISSER 'T HOOFT

Willem Adolph (handwritten annotation above printed name)

THE PRESSURE
OF
OUR COMMON CALLING

DOUBLEDAY & COMPANY, INC.
GARDEN CITY, NEW YORK
1959

LIBRARY OF CONGRESS CATALOG CARD NUMBER 59–12655
COPYRIGHT © 1959 BY W. A. VISSER 'T HOOFT
ALL RIGHTS RESERVED
PRINTED IN THE UNITED STATES OF AMERICA
FIRST EDITION

INTRODUCTORY NOTE

———◆———

DR. VISSER 'T HOOFT has kindly agreed that this book should be considered as one of the working documents to be used by the World's Student Christian Federation as preparatory studies for a world conference on The Life and Mission of the Church to be held in Strasbourg in July 1960, and for several other meetings, international and national, all part of the same general effort. I therefore wish to commend this book to all members of Student Christian Movements and to all friends of the Federation who wish to support this effort to study the missionary problems of our time and to prepare students to find their place of service in the total mission of the Church in the world.

I also wish to draw the attention of readers of this book to another publication which is to follow: five Bible studies prepared by Mademoiselle Françoise Florentin, Secretary of the French Student Christian Movement, to accompany the work of Dr. Visser 't Hooft and to give to Christian students and other Christian groups an opportunity to pursue his line of thinking through the study of the Scriptures. These five Bible study outlines can also be used very profitably for personal study. They will be published very shortly under the title: *Five Bible Study Outlines on The Life and Mission of the Church.*

Philippe Maury, GENERAL SECRETARY
WORLD'S STUDENT CHRISTIAN FEDERATION

PREFACE

In SEPTEMBER 1957 I had the privilege of giving the Taylor lectures in Yale Divinity School. Several of my colleagues on the staffs of the World Council of Churches and the World's Student Christian Federation read the manuscript and made constructively critical comments. In the light of these comments and of further reflection the lectures were largely rewritten and a good deal of new material added.

Since this is a book about the theology of the ecumenical movement, I must make it very clear that it represents in no sense an official statement of the standpoint of the World Council of Churches or any other ecumenical body. To those who know the World Council this will be obvious. But it happens often that others confuse the personal statements of an officer of the Council with statements of the Council itself. I have of course, tried to think in terms of the nature and task of the Council. But there remains a world of difference between that which one servant of the Council says and what all the churches in the Council say together. At the same time one cannot write about the underlying issues of the ecumenical movement without realizing strongly that we are still at the beginning of the discussion and that all we say on this subject must be very provisional. Nobody is "ready" with these new and difficult questions. This little book is, therefore, simply a contribution to an ongoing discussion.

W. A. Visser 't Hooft

CONTENTS

———◆———

THE PRESSURE
OF
OUR COMMON CALLING

I

HOW DOES
UNITY GROW?

———————◆◆———————

DIETRICH BONHOEFFER, whose life and witness was so wholly identified with the ecumenical movement and who had thought deeply about its true meaning, wrote in 1932: "There is as yet no theology of the ecumenical movement," and he continued: "Each time when the Church of Christ in history has arrived at a new understanding of its own nature, it has produced a theology which expresses that understanding adequately . . . If the ecumenical movement is based on a new understanding of the Church of Christ it will produce a theology. If it does not succeed in doing so, this will mean that it is nothing else than a purely utilitarian organisation."[1]

What would Bonhoeffer say about the ecumenical situation twenty-five years later if he could be with us? I believe that he would say something like this: "It is true that there has been a certain amount of progress in clarifying the nature and the objectives of the ecumenical movement. In such documents as the Toronto statement of 1950 on "The Church, the Churches and the World Council of Churches" and in the Evanston report on "Our Oneness in Christ and Our Disunity as Churches" we have answered a number of questions about the meaning of our ecumenical relationships. We know better than we knew before that the moti-

[1] *Die Eiche*, 1932, p. 334; also in *Gesammelte Schriften*, Band I, München, 1958, p. 140.

vating force of the ecumenical movement is the rediscovery of the Church as the Church of God rooted in the work of Christ, the indispensable instrument for the fulfillment of the divine plan, existing essentially as one single people gathered by the Holy Spirit. But that does not yet mean that we have a theology of the ecumenical *movement*. For this common consensus on the *nature* of the Church is in danger of remaining an abstraction unless we succeed in relating it to the concrete realities of our interchurch relationships. We need a theology which will help us to bridge the gulf between our theory and our practice—a theology which answers the questions: What is it that makes the ecumenical movement move? How does unity grow?

This would not be an unfair judgment. We have a wealth of literature on the issues of church unity, but this deals nearly exclusively with the question: What are the true characteristics of a united Church? Now this is obviously a fundamental problem which must find a common answer if the ecumenical movement is to reach its ultimate purpose. But it is not the only ecumenical problem. We must not be so exclusively concerned with the goal that we have no energy or time left for the planning and mapping of the road which will lead to the goal. A theology of the ecumenical movement must deal with the meaning of our *present* relationships. It must give guidance for that in-between period when we can no longer remain wholly isolated from each other and realize that we must stay together, but when we are not yet able to enter into that full fellowship with each other which would express itself in living together as members of one visible body.

We need such a theology of the ecumenical movement because a Christian movement without theology is like a ship without a rudder. The choices which must be made, the decisions which have to be taken imply assumptions about the task of the ecumenical movement. One cannot even draw up a budget for the World Council of Churches without theologizing. And if one acts without any realization that theological issues are involved, one is likely to follow non-theological principles which are only a nice expression for worldy motives.

We also need a theology for the ecumenical movement in order to arrive at clear common criteria by which we can evaluate its work, its utterances. At the present moment we are in the dangerous situation that ecumenical activities are often judged from a great variety of different standpoints, each of which represents a specific interest or hobby. Some who are actively engaged in ecumenical activities are exclusively concerned with the practical service which the World Council renders; others consider that nothing counts except the discussion of questions of faith and order; others again ask only whether the ecumenical movement promotes evangelism and missions; some see no other point in the existence of the movement than its work for international peace; some ask only whether the ecumenical study work produces worthy theological results. Thus we are in danger of producing a number of unrelated ecumenical operations without a commonly accepted strategy in which first things come first. Now it is impossible to arrive at clear criteria unless we work out a coherent conception of the total task of the ecumenical movement, and we cannot see that task as a whole until we succeed in answering the basic questions about its raison d'être and about the implications which its existence has for the life of the churches.

This applies equally to the various bodies which together make up the ecumenical movement. For all of them the question how they can best serve the main purpose of the movement is vital; for all of them it is essential to discover how Christian unity grows. In this matter there is no fundamental difference between the tasks of the World Council of Churches, of the International Missionary Council, of the confessional alliances, and of the "independent" Christian lay movements.

But is there no danger that a theology of the ecumenical movement will divide rather than unite? That danger exists. It is conceivable that by defining such a theology we may cut ourselves off from those who will not or cannot accept it. For that reason we have to be very careful not to declare that any particular theology is *the* theology of the ecumenical movement until it has been fully considered by all concerned. That applies also to this book, which is no more than a contribution to the ecumenical discussion on the subject. There is, however, even greater danger in refusing to face these basic issues. For such a refusal could only mean, as Bonhoeffer said, that we are not engaged in a common spiritual enterprise with common assumptions as to its meaning, but rather in a purely utilitarian effort of practical co-operation.

The basic issues of the theology of the ecumenical movement are: What is the nature of the relation which the churches have together in that movement? Is it a purely organizational relationship or is it an expression of a real unity? If the latter is true, how is that unity related to the unity of which the New Testament speaks? And how can that unity which we have already grow toward that full unity which is, according to New Testament teaching, an indispensable characteristic of the Church of Christ?

The paradox that churches which do not only differ from each other in matters of faith and order but disagree with each other about important points of doctrine, and in many cases do not have sacramental fellowship, are, nevertheless, able to work together and even to witness together in specific matters had, of course, occupied the thoughts of the pioneers of the ecumenical movement. The 1920 Encyclica of the Patriarchate of Constantinople,[2] which was of great importance for the thinking of the ecumenical movement in its first stage, had said that closer relationship and fellowship (*koinonia*) between the Christian churches was not prevented by the doctrinal differences existing between them and that such understanding would be in the interest of the whole Christian body and could prepare and facilitate "the complete blessed union" of the churches. In the following years leaders of the "Life and Work" movement formulated a more explicit answer to the fundamental question. This answer is contained in a letter which the leaders of the "Life and Work" movement sent to "Faith and Order" in 1922. This is the important passage: "The Bishop of Winchester has rightly said: 'that in the region of moral and social questions we desire all Christians to begin at once to act as if they were one body in one visible fellowship. This can be done by all alike without any injury to theological principles.' As Dr. Kapler has said: 'Doctrine divides, but service unites.' We are concerned with service, and we believe that by serving the co-operation of the churches we shall break down prejudices and create a spirit of fellowship which will render the accomplishment of the aims of the Faith and Order movement less difficult to achieve."[3]

[2]*Documents of Christian Unity*. A selection, 1955, London, p. 17.

[3]Söderblom, *The Church and Peace*, Burge Memorial Lecture, Oxford, 1929, p. 32. See also *A History of the Ecumenical Movement*, London, 1954, p. 572.

This theory of ecumenical action had first been formulated in 1918 in the report of the Church of England commission on "Christianity and Industrial Problems," a report submitted to the Archbishop of Canterbury. It had been taken over two years later in the report of the Lambeth Conference of Anglican bishops in a slightly stronger form: "We believe that there are no principles at stake which can rightly be held to hinder all denominations from beginning without delay to act as if they were wholly one body in the department of public, moral and social witness."[4]

In the following years this "as if" theory came to exert a widespread influence. Archbishop Nathan Söderblom used it again and again in order to explain and justify the "Life and Work" approach to Christian unity and stated as late as the year 1929 that "all" had "witnessed the correctness of this opinion."[5] Wilred Monod went so far as to describe the "as-if" method as the characteristic method of the Stockholm conference of 1925. He said: "We had recourse to the method advocated in psychology and spirituality: 'Act as if.' Go forward as if the Church of Christ here on earth were actually a united front."[6] At the Lausanne Conference Professor Balanos of Athens quoted the phrase with approval.[7]

At the first world conference on "Faith and Order" in 1927 the phrase became almost a part of the official conference findings. The report of the seventh section, which was submitted to that conference by Archbishop Söderblom, contained the following sentence: "In fulfilling the Master's law of love all Christians should act together as if they were one body in one visible fellowship without any injury to theological principles."[8] But this report was rejected and the new text written by Bishop Brent to replace it does not contain these or similar words.[9]

[4]Report, Lambeth Conference, 1920, pp. 74–75. See Bell, *Christian Unity: The Anglican Position*, 1948, p. 156.

[5]*The Church and Peace*, p. 32. See also *"Einigung der Christenheit,"* 1925, p. 218, and Söderblom's address at the Lausanne Faith and Order Conference. Official Report (German edition), p. 321.

[6]Quoted in Congar, *Divided Christendom*, 1937, p. 118.

[7]Report, Lausanne World Conference on Faith and Order (German edition), p. 506. He ascribed the words incorrectly to the Bishop of Manchester (William Temple).

[8]Report, p. 397.

[9]There is, however, nothing in the record of the conference to indicate that any delegate objected to the "as if" formula.

Now this widely accepted pragmatic approach (which curiously enough was not invented in the country which has so often been regarded as the country of pragmatism *par excellence,* but which came from the older churches) was in many ways a danger to the spiritual and theological health of the ecumenical movement. It is certainly true that Christians can speak and act on specific moral issues even if they are not at one about important matters of faith and order. And it is highly desirable that they should do so. It is also true that by so doing they may be drawn closer together. But such common action excluding the common consideration of the basis of action on such application of the Christian faith, and not attempting to agree as to the content of the Christian faith, is in no way comparable to the fellowship in Christ of which the New Testament speaks. For that fellowship is precisely a comprehensive fellowship which embraces faith and life, doctrine and service. To act together "as if" that fellowship had been established when, in reality, agreement is sought only in the realm of social principles is to create the wrong impression that a utilitarian relationship is an adequate response to the call which God addresses to His Church and to the need of the world. The answer is inadequate because it neglects the central ecumenical task of the Church, namely, to restore its unity in Christ. Co-operation is not unity. A consensus about social action combined with a moratorium on theological and doctrinal discussion leads easily to the conclusion that the churches have done enough when they have established co-operative relationships. But that is a false conclusion. For unity in Christ is unity in the deepest convictions and unity which embraces all of life. Those who accept co-operation as sufficient are in danger of retarding the growth of that true unity.

The "as if" answer is also inadequate because it fails to take account of the importance of theological agreement for action itself. Common action which is not based on common convictions cannot deal with the deepest needs of society. Action which is not controlled and purified by the eternal truth of the gospel can easily degenerate and become the defense of ideological interests rather than of specifically Christian concerns. It is, therefore, impossible to separate faith from life, or theology from moral action. Dr. J. H. Oldham, whose keen and penetrating mind shaped the program and content of the second Life and Work Conference at Oxford in 1937, wrote just before that conference: "The chief need of the Church to-day to equip it to fulfil its mission to society is theology."[10] And Oxford, 1937, proved that, by putting the issue of the Christian attitude to the state, to the nation, and to society in the framework of central Christian doctrine, the ecumenical movement gained in clarity, in spiritual authority, and in relevance to the modern world.

It is, therefore, not surprising that the "as if" method created grave misunderstanding of the nature of the ecumenical movement. Some went so far as to state that this kind of ecumenism did not arise from supernatural faith but from merely human considerations, and that, instead of being concerned with unity of belief, "Life and Work" was concerned only with "the moral attitude common to all the sects and underlying the variety and contrariety of their creeds."[11] This was, of course, an unfair judgment, for the great majority of the advocates of the "as if" method never meant to apply their method as a general theological principle. It was for them a provisional solution of a difficult practical problem. But the fact remains that they made it easy to interpret the ecumenical movement in terms of doctrinal relativism.

Were the pioneers, then, wholly wrong? In the perspective of all that we have learned since those early days we can see that they were in fact seeking to express an important truth which belongs to the heart of the ecumenical experience, but which need not be formulated in such a misleading way. They had themselves expressed their meaning much more adequately when they had given the "Life and Work" movement the title, *communio in serviendo ecumenica* (ecumenical communion in serving), for that title made it clear that in serving our Lord and in rendering service to the world, they were brought together in an ecumenical fellowship which, while far from being an adequate manifestation of the one Church of Christ, was, nevertheless, a real witness to the gathering work of Christ. Again the Encyclica of the Ecumenical Patriarchate of 1920 had said: "We consider as the most important thing that love between the

[10]*The Church and Its Function in Society*, London, 1937, p. 163.

[11]Congar, *Divided Christendom*, London, 1939, p. 120. See also Journet, *L'Unité de l'Eglise*, Paris, 1927, p. 83.

churches must be revived and strengthened so that they may no longer look upon each other as strangers and enemies, but as relatives and friends in Christ and as 'fellow heirs, members of the same body, and partakers of the promise in Christ Jesus through the gospel'" (Eph. 3:6). And this also implied that by living together the life of Christian agape, both in their relations with each other and in their relations with the world, the churches could begin to rediscover that unity which is rooted in the fact that Christ's work embraces them all. Archbishop Nathan Söderblom, speaking at the Lausanne Conference in 1927, applied Pascal's famous words to the ecumenical situation, "You would not seek me if you had not already found me," and said that the very seeking after a fuller joint expression of unity indicated that we had already at the bottom of our Christian experience such a unity. In other words, Söderblom and his colleagues were really seeking to give expression to the conviction that there existed a real unity and that that unity could become more explicit if the churches would seek to fulfill together the mission given to the Church by its Lord.

In 1937 when the "Life and Work" and "Faith and Order" movements held their second world conferences, the time had come to formulate a clearer answer to the question of the nature of the ecumenical movement. "Life and Work," at Oxford under Oldham's leadership, took its stand on the conviction that "the real crisis of the Church relates not to its social programme but to its faith."[12] The conference message (written by Archbishop William Temple) spoke boldly of "our unity in Christ" as "an experienced fact, not a theme of aspiration," and based on "the redeeming acts of the one Lord of the Church." And it was again Archbishop Temple who said in the opening sermon of the Faith and Order Conference at Edinburgh: "We could not seek union if we did not already possess unity. . . . It is because we are one in allegiance to one Lord that we seek and hope for the way of manifesting that unity in our witness to Him before the world."[13] In other words, we need no "as if"; we can say thank-

[12]Oldham in *The Church and Its Function in Society*, London, 1937, p. 105.

[13]Report, Faith and Order Conference, Edinburgh, 1937, London, 1938, p. 21.

fully "because." The ecumenical task is not a hopeless task because Jesus Christ is gathering us together.

Some years later William Paton, who at that time served both the International Missionary Council and the World Council of Churches, struggled with the same problem of the unity already given and the unity to be achieved. In the so-called Paton memorandum of 1941, addressed to the churches and missions of India, he raised the question whether churches which desired to be united could not act in all possible matters in the same way as they should if there were a united Church in being. This formulation was much less open to criticism. For he explained his proposal in this way: "It is possible in view of the ascertained large measure of agreement between the churches, to proceed at this time of urgency to act in virtue of that agreement so far as it extends."[14] In other words, that unity which already exists must be allowed to have its full effect. It is not enough to discuss plans of reunion; we must also expose ourselves right now to those forces which make for unity, and that means living and acting together on the basis of the convictions which we already have in common.

Ecumenical history teaches us, therefore, that we must learn to distinguish between the unity which exists and the fuller unity which should characterize the Church of Christ and which it is our task to realize. There is the unity which holds us together right now and obliges us to go forward together. And there is the unity which is promised to us and which will be given to us in God's time if we respond obediently to His work of gathering. There is the unity of the road and there is the unity of the goal.

Thus, by the time when the plan to establish the World Council of Churches was formed, the fourteen signatories of the "Letter of Invitation" said: "It is not only or chiefly because it may be practical convenience and utility that we commend this scheme. Rather it is because the very nature of the Church demands that it shall make manifest to the world the unity in Christ of all who believe in Him. The full unity of the Church is something for which we must still work and pray. But there exists a unity in allegiance to our Lord for the manifestation of which we are

[14] *International Review of Missions*, 1941, p. 506.

responsible. We may not pretend that the existing unity among Christians is greater than in fact it is; but we should act upon it so far as it is already a reality."[15]

The basic problem of the ecumenical movement lies in that last phrase. There exists already a real unity. The churches would not have declared (as they did at the first assembly of the World Council of Churches) that they did intend to stay together if they were not aware of a real bond between them, the bond of their common faith in Jesus Christ as God and Savior, the bond of their common calling. The Amsterdam message describes that unity in these words: "We are divided from one another, but Christ has made us His own and He is not divided." In a resolution concerning the nature of the World Council, also adopted by the first assembly, it was said of the churches: "They find their unity in Him. They have not to create their unity; it is the gift of God." Again, when in 1950 an attempt was made to define the ecclesiological significance of the World Council in the Toronto statement on "The Church, the Churches and the World Council of Churches," it was underlined that "a very real unity has been discovered in ecumenical meetings which is, to all who collaborate in the World Council, the most precious element of its life."[16]

This already existing unity enables the World Council to be a channel for common witness and action of the churches in those matters in which they have come to a common mind. There are areas in which a substantial common witness has been given; there are others in which this has not been possible. But we may say that there is reason for deep gratitude that, in the short period of its life, the World Council has been allowed to manifest such a large degree of unity among the churches.

It is, however, essential that we do not pretend that the existing

[15]*The World Council of Churches. Its Process of Formation*, 1946, pp. 172–73. The letter was drafted by Archbishop Temple.

[16]Compare also "A Word to the Churches" from the third World Conference on Faith and Order, Lund, 1952: "As we have come to know one another better our eyes have been opened to the depth and pain of our separations and also to our fundamental unity. The measure of unity which it has been given to the Churches to experience together must now find clearer manifestation. A faith in the one Church of Christ which is not implemented by *acts* of obedience is dead. There are truths about the nature of God and His Church which will remain for ever closed to us unless we act together in obedience to the unity which is already ours."

unity is greater than, in fact, it is. We must not speak, as happens too often, as if the ecumenical movement can properly be called "the World Church." For that terminology gives the impression that what we have today in the World Council is the definite and sufficient answer to the problem of Christian unity. In fact the World Council is only the provisional solution of that problem, or, in the words of Bishop Lesslie Newbigin, "a transitory phase of the journey from disunity to unity."[17]

The unity which we have is real, but it is not to be identified with that unity which, according to the New Testament, belongs to the nature of the Church of Christ and existed in fact in the New Testament Church. This is so because the unity which we have in the World Council does not imply full sacramental communion between the churches. It is so because there exist differences in the realms of doctrine and witness which are not merely various expressions of our basic gospel, such as we find in the New Testament, but which contradict each other. It is so because we have our self-contained confessional and denominational structures, so that even churches which are willing to have full sacramental communion with each other, nevertheless, continue to live as separate entities and do not manifest unity at the decisive level of the local congregation or parish.

It must, of course, be added that there is a further respect in which our present unity is not comparable to the unity of the early Church. That unity included all who called upon the name of Christ. The unity we have in the ecumenical movement embraces many churches, but there are also a number of large churches which do not share in it. In other words, the ecumenical movement is far from being fully ecumenical.

Now it is, of course, true that the New Testament Church also had to cope with divisive tendencies, but these tendencies were never allowed to harden into self-sufficient organizational units. It seems to me that Professor John Knox, in his book on *The Early Church and The Coming Great Church*,[18] with its strong emphasis on the existence of these divisions, has at the same time shown us that these divisions were never accepted and justified

[17]*The Household of God*, London, 1953, p. 21.

[18]New York, 1955.

because the thought of a plurality of peoples of God was as unthinkable as that of a plurality of saviors. In a penetrating study on this subject,[19] Professor Oscar Cullman calls attention to the remarkable fact that the very real divisive tendencies in the early Church never led to a real break or to the creation of church bodies separated from each other. He gives four reasons for this: the general realization that the Church must be one; the energetic resistance against ecclesiastical parties; the readiness to make concessions whenever this could be done without giving up fundamental convictions; the bond of love as expressed in interchurch aid, particularly the aid for the poor of Jerusalem.

We cannot possibly maintain that the unity which we have today in the World Council has reached the point at which it corresponds to that picture. The realization that the Church must be one because of its very nature and mission has not penetrated into the whole life of our churches; we are not yet thoroughly ashamed of our many "parties"; there is little readiness to make a sacrifice for the cause of unity. Only with regard to interchurch aid is our record perhaps somewhat comparable to that of the early church.

Our present unity in the ecumenical movement cannot be considered as the unity which the Church is meant to have, because the continued existence of separate churches which do not only show a great variety (such as should characterize the life of the body of Christ) but also real divergence and disagreement contradicts the central truth of the oneness of the Church of Christ. At present our ecumenical relationships manifest unity, but the visible expressions of our church life obscure that unity. The World Council of Churches is not the adequate answer to the problem of disunity. The adequate answer cannot be a council of churches which are not yet ready to be united. That answer must simply be the one Church of Christ.

So we must neither underestimate nor overestimate our present unity. It is a real point of departure; but it is only a point of departure. If we do not recognize and accept gratefully the great gift of God, which is the unity which we have already, we will never be able to receive the greater gift of the full unity which is in store for us. On the other hand, if we believe that we have

[19]*Das Urchristentum und das ökumenische Problem. Kirchenblatt für die Reformierte Schweiz,* February 21, 1957.

already found the unity which the Church is meant to have, we deny that the word of God really means what it says about full unity in Christ. The two temptations of the ecumenical life prove to be the same as those of the Christian life in general: on the one hand, lack of gratitude for that which God does for us; on the other hand, anticipation of the fulfillment of God's promise.

The real issue, then, is how our present unity can *grow* toward the unity which is biblically normal. So far we have not given sufficient attention to that question. Thus the most substantial statement on the significance of the World Council, the Toronto statement of 1950 on "The Church, the Churches and the World Council of Churches," is drawn up to answer the question: What *is* the World Council of Churches? rather than the even more important question: How can the World Council of Churches help the churches in their growing together until they reach the fuller unity? This was inevitable at the time, for the World Council had first to explain what membership in the World Council did mean and did not mean for the member churches. But the time has now come to ask that second question and to concentrate on the issue of the *growth* of Christian unity. "Toronto" had stated that membership in the World Council does not imply the acceptance of a specific doctrine concerning the nature of church unity. But it had also said: "The Council stands for church unity." In other words, the Council must, by its very nature, remain neutral with regard to the precise form which unity must take. That remains wholly a matter to be decided by the churches themselves. But the Council believes that there must be real and manifest unity, and that implies that it believes in the *growth* of unity and in its own obligation to further that growth. In this its purpose is not to magnify itself—on the contrary, the achievement of real unity would make the Council's existence superfluous—but to help the churches to live and witness as the one Church of Christ.

How does Christian unity grow? The answer is given in the key word of the classical passage on unity: Ephesians 4. That key word is: calling. The unity of the Church is the necessary corollary to its calling. The Church is the community of those who are called (1 Cor. 1:23). It can simply be described as "the called" (Jude 1). And the word *ekklesia* means the body of those who are called out.[20] Thus, in the New Testament, calling does not refer primarily to individual callings, or vocations, but to the common calling in Christ (Rom. 8:30, 2 Tim. 1:9). And it is this common calling which binds the Christians together in an indestructible fellowship. They are united because they "share in a heavenly call" (Heb. 3:1). And there is one body because it can be said of them: "You were called to the one hope that belongs to your call" (Eph. 4:4).

This calling is not a privilege to be enjoyed; it demands constantly renewed response. It must be confirmed, implemented (2 Pet. 1:10). Christians are exhorted to lead a life worthy of their calling (Eph. 4:1).

God unites those whom He calls. And the unity of the called is realized as they live up to their calling. Unity grows, therefore, as they become more deeply aware of and more obedient to their calling. In the same way, church unity grows whenever and wherever the churches expose themselves to the pressure of their common calling and live worthy of that common calling.

In the New Testament, unity is never static. Unity is always the result of the gathering, upbuilding, perfecting work of the Lord of the Church. He is the creator of all real unity. Unity grows when and where the Church puts itself wholly at His disposal. Unity is weakened when and where the Church seek its own ends and the parts do not "work properly" (Eph. 4:16), that is, where they do not fulfill their God-given calling. When this is true of the growth of such unity as existed in the New Testament Church, it is equally true of the growth of the unity which we have already among the churches in the ecumenical movement. There is no way for churches which are neither fully united nor completely separated to arrive at real, concrete, manifest unity except the way of common obedience to the common calling. The ecumenical task is to go forward together in making a common response to the one calling.

This must, of course, not be taken to mean that any church at any time is to be forced to participate in any action, in any common utterance which it considers to be in conflict with the truth and the will of God. To act on the unity which exists already, to work toward the growth of that unity does not imply

[20]Significat ecclesia evocationem (Catechismus Romanus 1:10:2).

that any pressure is brought upon the churches other than the pressure which is inherent in the common calling and to which every church must make its own free response.

But then there is no need for any human, organizational pressure once it is realized what the common calling really means and once the churches are, in fact, seeking to become worthy of that calling. It is only when the churches are introverted and self-centered or when they seek the glory of man rather than the glory of God that the question of unity is seen as a debatable issue. Once churches are again *in via*, once they remember their character as a pilgrim people which seek the eternal city, they are naturally concerned with their unity as they are with their calling.

Bishop Lesslie Newbigin has underlined that when Christians are engaged in the task of missionary obedience they are in the situation in which the Church is truly the Church and that, in that situation, the disunity which is easily taken for granted among churches which are not in a missionary situation becomes literally intolerable, because it is felt to contradict the whole nature of the apostolic mission at its heart.[21] This is profoundly true, but it must be applied to the total mission of the Church, which includes not only its missionary outreach in the technical sense of that word but all aspects of its calling.

Thus the theme of the ecumenical movement is not unity as an isolated goal; it is unity as the outcome of the common effort to express the integrity and the wholeness of the Church of Christ. It is unity through renewal. Nikolaus L. Zinzendorf, that ecumenical theologian *avant la lettre*, had seen this already: "All fellowship [*gemeinschaft*] which is only based on agreement of opinions and forms without a change of heart, is a dangerous sect."[22]

The ecumenical movement does not owe its origin to a passion for unity alone. Its roots lie in a rediscovery of the nature and mission of the Church of Christ. Nothing less than that could have created the movement; nothing less than that can keep it going and growing. A theology of the ecumenical movement must,

[21]*The Household of God*, London, 1953, p. 151.

[22]Quoted by Wallau, *Die Einigung der Kirchen*, 1925, p. 267.

therefore, be concerned with the whole calling of the Church and seek to answer the question what implications that calling has for the relationships which the churches should have with each other in the ecumenical movement and for the tasks which they should undertake together.

What is the whole calling of the Church? It is to fulfill the mission with which it has been entrusted by Christ. "As thou didst send me into the world, so I have sent them into the world" (Jn. 17:18). That mission can neither be wholly identified with nor separated from the mission of Christ Himself. To identify it with the mission of Christ is to forget the uniqueness of His work and ministry, to separate it from the mission of Christ is to deny His continued presence in and with His Church. "The ministry of the Church is related to the ministry of Christ in such a way that in and through the ministry of the Church it is always Christ Himself who is at work, nourishing, sustaining, ordering and governing His Church on earth."[23] It follows that "the pattern of Jesus' ministry remains the pattern of the Church's ministry"[24] or that "the shape of His life is the shape of the Church's life."[25]

Now the several aspects of the work of Christ and, therefore, also of the calling of the Church are described in various ways in the New Testament. It is possible to speak of *marturia* (witness), *oikonomia* (stewardship), and *diakonia* (service), or of *leitourgia* (worship), *diakonia*, and *marturia*, or of the royal, sacerdotal, and prophetic ministry. We choose three aspects of the mission of the Church which seem to us more fundamental than any others and to include the other aspects which have been mentioned. These three are: *marturia*, or witness; *diakonia*, or service; and *koinonia*, or fellowship. We may refer in this connection to the calling of the disciples. The Gospel of Mark 3:14-15 says simply: "He appointed twelve, to be with him [koinonia], and to be sent out to preach [marturia] and have authority to cast out demons" [diakonia]. We can also link those three forms of the mission to the classical conception of the three offices of Christ: the prophetic office which

[23]Torrance, *Royal Priesthood*, Edinburgh, 1955, p. 37. See also Schweizer, *Das Leben des Herrn in der Gemeinde und ihren Diensten*, 1946.

[24]Paul Minear in *Work and Vocation*, New York, 1954.

[25]Report of the third World Conference on Faith and Order, Lund, p. 22.

corresponds to marturia, the priestly office which corresponds to koinonia, and the royal office which, in the revolutionary conception of the New Testament, corresponds to diakonia. It should be explained that we do not use the term "mission" for one aspect of the calling of the Church because we believe that it has to do with the *whole* calling of the Church.[26]

These three aspects of the mission of the Church have in common that each can be used to describe the whole work and life of the Church, but that each has also a more specific meaning and can refer to one particular task of the Church. The whole life of the Church must express its witnessing character, and its service and fellowship are aspects of its witness. But, in the same way, the whole life of the Church is service, and through its witness and fellowship the Church renders service to the world. Or again, the whole life of the Church must express its character as a unique form of fellowship, and its witness and service must be witness and service in fellowship. Biblical language does not draw such sharp demarcation lines as we are accustomed to do. These three aspects of the calling are interrelated but not identical. They are entrances to one and the same sacred building. Each leads to the center, but each allows us to contemplate the interior of the building from a different angle.

[26]In the New Testament, "apostole" is used only four times and then in the "technical" sense of "apostleship." On the other hand, "apostellein," or "pepein" (= to send) is used most often of the sending of Jesus Himself and is the comprehensive expression for the whole work of Christ and of His Church in the world.

II

THE CALLING TO
WITNESS

———◆———

How is the Word of God transmitted to men? Most of us are
inclined to answer: by preaching. For that is the expression which
we find so very often in our translations of the New Testament and
that is the traditional way in which the Church carries on its ministry. But the expression is in many ways misleading. For it over-
simplifies the biblical situation. The New Testament has some
thirty different words for the ministry of the Word and each has
its own specific shade of meaning.[1] At the same time, what we
generally mean by preaching—the systematic discourse in which,
on the basis of a biblical text, a specific doctrinal or edifying theme
is developed—is something very different from what the New
Testament expresses in these varied words.

We cannot deal with all of these expressions. But we choose the
three most representative, namely *kerussein, euaggelizesthai,* and
marturein. The first is specially used by the Synoptics and by St.
Paul, the second by St. Luke and St. Paul. Marturein is a specifically
Johannine expression.

Kerussein means, literally, heralding.[2] In the ancient Greek world
the herald is the duly accredited emissary of a ruler, who enjoys a

[1]Friedrich in Kittel, *Wörterbuch zum N.T.* III:702.

[2]See Kerussein in Kittel, *W.N.T.* and Karl Barth, *Kirchliche Dogmatik*
IV:2:223.

number of the privileges to which his lord is entitled. His one and only task is to transmit in the most faithful and clearest manner the message entrusted to him. The herald could also play a role in the religious life of the city and say public prayers. Stoic philosophers called themselves heralds of God. But it is interesting to note that the New Testament does not speak often of heralds, but very often of heralding. This is surely due to the fact that the "kerygma," the message, is considered so much more important than the herald himself and that the New Testament herald is in no way entitled to those privileges which were given to the heralds of the ancient Greek world.

Euaggelizesthai means to announce good tidings. The evangelist of Greek civilization is the messenger who announces a victory or another historic event in the life of the empire or of its ruler. It is not surprising that this term was used in the Septuagint to describe the joyful tidings of God's decisive intervention in the life of Israel. Thus Isaiah speaks of the "evangelizer" who announces the victory of God and thus inaugurates the new day. When he proclaims, "Your God reigns" (Is. 52:7), the time of salvation, of the great peace between God and man, has actually arrived. The coming of Jesus, who announces the arrival of the kingdom, is the fulfillment of this prophecy (Acts 10:36). He is both the evangelizer who proclaims the good news to the poor (Is. 61:1, Mt. 11:5, Lk. 4:18) and the evangel itself (Mk. 1:1, Mk. 14:9).[3]

Marturein, or witnessing is an expression with a definitely juridical background. The eyewitness plays a decisive role in the trial. His task is to tell the court exactly what has happened, that is, the truth and nothing but the truth. The later transition of meaning from eyewitness to "martyr," in the sense of witness who confirms his confession by his suffering or death, is foreshadowed but not explicitly stated in the New Testament.

But our concern is not, in the first place, with the different shades of meaning of these three expressions. The more important question is what they have in common, for an answer to that question will help us understand the specific task of the Church.

It seems to me that the following five points are specially significant:

[3]Mk. 14:9, in connection with Mk. 14:8, shows that the evangel is not only the evangel of Jesus but especially the evangel about Jesus.

1. In the first place, all heralding, evangelizing, and witnessing are based on a specific *mandate.* St. Paul puts the question sharply: "How can men preach [herald] unless they are sent?" (Rom. 10:15). St. Paul himself is an evangelist because he is recruited by the Lord. "Necessity is laid upon me. Woe to me if I do not evangelize" (1 Cor. 9:16). But the same is true of the first disciples: "He appointed twelve, to be with him, and to be sent out to preach" [herald] (Mk. 3:14, cf. Mt. 10:5-7). And the risen Lord gives the specific mandate to His apostles to herald the gospel (Mk. 16:15) and to be his witnesses (*marturs*) to the ends of the earth (Acts 1:8).

The Apostolate

It is not merely that they are called to talk about Jesus. It is rather that they are to participate in God's work in Christ. For God Himself evangelizes. St. Peter speaks of God preaching good news of peace by Jesus Christ (Acts 10:36). And Jesus' own ministry was to bring the evangel of peace (Eph. 2:17). Similarly he came to herald the coming of the kingdom (Mt. 4:17) and in order to witness (marturein) to the truth (cf. Rev. 1:5). If, then, men are sent out to preach, they become wholly involved in a divine enterprise. They do not speak only about Christ, but in His name. They are ambassadors for Christ (2 Cor. 5:20), and God makes His appeal through them.

2. In the second place, the three key words imply that the function of the speaker is wholly *instrumental*. He is not to produce his own ideas or impressions. "What we preach [herald] is not ourselves," says St. Paul (2 Cor. 4:5). He is to report objectively. The one duty of the herald and the messenger of good news is to proclaim the great message entrusted to them. The eyewitness is to give a faithful account of what he has seen. "That which was from the beginning, which we have heard, which we have seen with our own eyes, which we have looked upon and touched with our hands, concerning the word of life——the life was made manifest, and we saw it, and we testify [marturein] to it. . ." (1 Jn. 1:1-2). "For we cannot but speak of what we have seen and heard," say St. Peter and St. John (Acts 4:20). And St. Paul receives the mandate to be a witness (martur) of what he has seen and heard (Acts 22:15).

3. In the third place, the content of the speaker's report has to do with *events*. At Pentecost the people hear the apostles speak of the *megalaia*, the mighty works, the great deeds of God (Acts 2:11). What are these deeds? They are the various stages in the unfolding of the one divine plan which has its center in the coming of Jesus Christ. The emphases differ according to the standpoint from which the books are written. The synoptics underline that the kingdom is at hand; St. John that the word has become flesh; St. Paul gives "first importance" to "what he received," namely, that Christ died, that He was buried, and He was raised (1 Cor. 15: 3–5). But there is no real difference. For all agree that what is to be heralded, proclaimed as good news, and witnessed to is the fact of the coming of Jesus Christ and its absolutely revolutionary implications for the life of man. There are not many gospels: a gospel about the kingdom, another one about the incarnate word, again another one about the cross and the resurrection. There is one single gospel, for Christ *is* the kingdom; He is the Word become flesh; He is the crucified and risen Lord.

4. In the fourth place, the purpose of the speaker's message is to urge upon his hearers that the events which he reports are of *decisive significance* for their life and that they must make an immediate decision with regard to them. The conclusion of every single witness is: repent, change around, turn to God. For this event is a challenge and an invitation. It is "now" that God commands men everywhere to repent, as St. Paul says on the Areopagus (Acts 17:30). Or, as he speaks elsewhere, "We are ambassadors for Christ, God making his appeal through us. We beseech you on behalf of Christ, be reconciled to God" (2 Cor. 5:20).

5. In the fifth place, the message given is a *public* message addressed to all who have ears to hear. It is destined to become a universal word of salvation. "This gospel of the kingdom will be preached [heralded] throughout the whole world [Oikoumene], as a testimony [marturion] to all nations" (Mt. 24:14, cf. Mk. 13:10). "Go into all the world and preach [herald] the gospel to the whole creation" (Mk. 16:15). "You shall be my witnesses [martures] in Jerusalem and in all Judea and Samaria and to the end of the earth" (Acts 1:8, cf. Lk. 24:47). Ananias explains the call which has come to St. Paul by saying: "You will be a witness for him to all men" (Acts 22:15). It is this absolute certainty of the world-wide universal validity of the gospel which leads St. Paul

to the startling anticipation expressed in Colossians 1:23: "The gospel which you heard, which has been preached [kerussein] to every creature under heaven."

The full implications of these various aspects of the ministry of the word become clear at the time of Pentecost. For through the outpouring of the Holy Spirit the apostolic community receives the power to become a missionary community. Pentecost represents, as it were, the enabling act by which the church becomes a witnessing body.

The universal witness is the result of the gift of the Holy Spirit, which constitutes the new people of God. For the Holy Spirit is a witnessing spirit. According to Luke 24:22–49, the risen Christ appoints His disciples as witnesses (martures) to all nations, but tells them to wait in Jerusalem until they will be clothed with power from on high. Similarly in Acts 1:8 the witness to the ends of the earth is described as the consequence of the coming of the Holy Spirit (cf. Jn. 20: 21–22). And this is also the central emphasis in the story of Pentecost: The promise is now fulfilled; the power from on high descends upon the disciples. They are now able to proclaim the gospel with authority; the Church is constituted, and it is from the very outset a witnessing Church.

On the day of Pentecost the Church comes into being as a community which has its very raison d'être in the universal proclamation of the gospel of Christ. It is not so that what we think of as the Church and what we think of as the missionary movement happen to be born on the same day. It is rather that they are fundamentally and originally one and the same reality.

It is one of the most certain results of biblical theology that, according to the New Testament, the very meaning of the period between the ascension of Christ and His return is that it provides the opportunity for the proclamation of the gospel to the whole world. The calling of the Church is to make full use of that opportunity. The preaching of the gospel to all the nations is itself a sign of that final period of history which began with the coming of Christ. St. Mark says (in the setting of a passage on the events which will characterize the "last" days) that "the gospel must first be preached to all nations" (13:10). And that "must" indicates that this belongs to the divine plan. Werner G. Kümmel (*Verheissung und Erfüllung*, Basel, 1945) and other scholars consider that this saying is not to be attributed to Jesus Himself, but is rather a projection of the missionary concern of the early church. I believe with Schniewind, in his commentaries on Matthew and Mark (on Mt. 24:14 and Mk. 13:10), that this is a saying of Jesus Himself which reflects the expectation so deeply rooted in the proclamation of Deutero-Isaiah that the good news of God's reign will in the last days be proclaimed to all the nations. (Is. 42:6, 49:6, 60:6). Thus it can be said that "the mission of the Church is in itself the eschatological dimension of the Church, indicating and signifying that the Church is not an end in herself, but that Christ and His reign was and is and will be the end."[4] The Church is the community which has been gathered and mobilized by the Holy Spirit in order to fulfill that part of the plan of God which must be fulfilled in the final period of history. The whole Church is, therefore, at all times called to be a witnessing Church.

The universal character of the witness is based on its eschatological character. The Old Testament prophets, and very particularly Deutero-Isaiah, had taught that in the end all nations would hear the good news of the reign of God. Thus we read in Isaiah 49:6: "It is too light a thing that you should be my servant to raise up the tribes of Jacob and to restore the preserved of Israel; I will give you as a light to the nations, that my salvation may reach to the end of the earth." We find an echo of these words when Jesus says to the disciples that the time is approaching when the Holy Spirit will be given to them, the spirit which is the power of the new, the "last" period of history, and that they will then become his witnesses in Jerusalem and in all Judea and Samaria and "to the end of the earth" (Acts 1:8). The next chapter of the Acts of the Apostles describes that great moment in terms of the end of time (Acts 2:17). The same word is used for the end of time as was used for the end of the earth (*eschatos*). Thus, as Dr. H. Hoekendijk has put it, "the end of the earth and the end of time belong together." If the Church is to fulfill its calling, it is not enough, or to use the words of Isaiah, "it is too light a thing" that it should be concerned

[4]Heinrich Meyer in *The Lutheran World*, Autumn, 1955.

with the witness in its immediate environment. For, as St. Paul said in the synagogue of Antioch of Pisidia: "So the Lord has commanded us, saying, 'I have set you to be a light for the Gentiles, that you may bring salvation to the uttermost [eschatos] parts of the earth'" (Acts 13:47). The Church, and every part of it, is only then truly the Church if it participates in the world-wide witnessing task, or, to put it in modern terms, "foreign mission." This going out, the crossing of national, continental, and cultural frontiers[5] to carry the gospel to those who have not heard it, is not an invention of a Western Christian civilization eager for expansion. Even though it may often have given the impression of being just an historically conditioned cultural rather than a basically Christian enterprise, it is in essence a requirement of the gospel itself and an obligation resting on every church in the world.

Unity grows as churches take seriously their common calling to witness. Why is this so? The first reason can best be formulated in a negative manner. Churches which are characterized by self-centered denominationalism and institutionalism cannot possibly fulfill their ecumenical calling. There is no greater obstacle to Christian unity than ecclesiastical introversion. A church which concentrates on the maintenance of its own life becomes the victim of the powerful social laws which govern the life of human institutions. Its main preoccupation becomes self-perpetuation. There is no earthly reason why churches which consider their own existence consciously or unconsciously as an end in itself should seek to become united with each other. The pull toward self-preservation will, in the long run, always be stronger than the pull toward unity. It is only when the whole life of the Church is seen, in the light of the whole plan of God, that the perspective begins to change. For if the Church exists in order to witness, if mission belongs to its very essence, then the question arises what is the specific place of each particular church in this world-embracing task. Sooner or later a

[5]The crossing of social frontiers belongs equally to the witnessing task of the Church, very especially in situations such as we have today in many so-called Christian countries in which the Church has become identified with one class or one ideology. But that necessary part of the Church's obedience must never be used as an excuse for unwillingness to go out and to participate in the mission to other peoples.

witnessing church finds itself confronted with the question of its relation to other churches engaged in one and the same calling.

At this point the objection may be raised that, in actual fact, churches with a strong missionary consciousness are often lacking in a true concern for co-operation and unity. We must admit that the experience of the ecumenical movement in this matter is contradictory. We have, on the one hand, the fact that the roots of the ecumenical movement are to be found in the missionary movement. The missionary strategist John R. Mott took the initiative for the Edinburgh Missionary Conference of 1910 which marked the beginning of the modern ecumenical movement. The missionary bishop Charles Brent became the founder of "Faith and Order." The most far-reaching schemes of reunion have been worked out in Asia and are largely motivated by evangelistic concerns.

But there is at the same time the fact that there are a number of churches, sects, and movements which are animated by a great passion to evangelize, but which are not ready to participate in the ecumenical movement of the churches, and, in many cases, even unwilling to have fellowship with any other Christian bodies. It is a well-known fact that in certain parts of the world the presence of a large number of missionaries from bodies which do not co-operate with the churches has become a major problem.

Two remarks should be made about this situation. The first is that one reason for the attitude of suspicion to the churches organized in the ecumenical movement is often that these churches are not considered as truly evangelistic and as deeply committed to the missionary task. It is therefore feared that the unity which the World Council promotes will in fact turn out to be the static institutional unity of the self-centered church rather than the dynamic unity of churches which fulfill their common missionary calling.

As the churches in the ecumenical movement accept increasingly that witness is not the calling of some of their members, that missions are not the concern of certain specialized groups but the calling of the Church as a whole and of all its parts, we may hope that a great deal of the suspicion against the ecumenical movement will disappear. So, in this respect also, a true commitment to mission can help the cause of unity.

Our second remark must be that just as it is possible to idolize other aspects of the calling of the Church, so it is possible to idolize its witness. The calling to witness can lead only to unity if those engaged in it let their eyes be opened to the total calling of the Church and listen as carefully to all that the Word of God has to say about unity and service as to what it says about witness. In such matters as the relations between older and younger churches or of proselytism among members of another denomination, it is not enough to insist on the duty of the Church to evangelize; it is equally necessary to remember its obligation to manifest the nature of Christian fellowship.

Another reason why witness can contribute to unity is that churches which accept the missionary mandate are brought back to those central objective realities of the faith which constitute the common witness of the whole Christian Church.

The missionary situation obliges each church to ask once again: Wherein lies the authority of the message which we proclaim? As the evangelist or missionary is confronted by other coherent systems of the truth and by other religions with ancient yet amazingly vital forms of spiritual life, it becomes clear that he cannot possibly justify his role simply by offering another variety of religious experience or by sharing certain spiritual values. The only good reason for the Christian witness proves to be that it is a witness to the *magnalia Dei*, the great and decisive deeds of God with their center in the sending of His Son. Thus the missionary situation throws the Church back on the central facts which are the foundation of the kerygma. To become engaged in the mission to the non-Christian world, whether in the West or in the East, is to receive a new sense of proportions. The great essential truths become greater and the secondary issues become smaller. But that means, at the same time, that we are thrown back on those elements of the witness which constitute the faith once delivered to the saints and which provide the substance of our unity. In the light of the encounter with a syncretistic religiosity such as dominates in Asia (but not only in Asia), or a messianic totalitarianism such as we confront in communism, or a humanistic relativism such as pervades our thinking in the West (but not only in the West), the points in which the churches differ no longer appear to be of primary importance, and we are obliged to proclaim the simple and central word concerning the incarnation, the cross, the resurrection.

St. Paul has a striking phrase to which most of our translations do not do justice. Again and again he tells the faithful that they should "*to auto phronein*." That is more than "being of the same mind" or "to agree with one another," as the RSV and other translations have it. It means to be concerned about one and the same thing, to ponder the thing which *is* the same and *means* the same to all of them. The phrase occurs twice in the Philippians, twice in Romans, once in the second epistle to the Corinthians.[6] It has clearly an objective reference. It points, as becomes clear in Philippians 2:3, to the one central *fact*, which is described in the christological hymn (Phil. 2:5–11), that is, the humiliation and glorification of the Servant of God, Jesus Christ. In Romans 15:5, the necessity of concentration on the one kerygma is underlined three times. A literal translation would read: "May the God of steadfastness and encouragement grant you to be concerned with one and the same thing in each other in accordance with Christ Jesus, in order that with one mind and with one voice you may glorify the God and Father of our Lord Jesus Christ."

A further point about the relation of witness to unity is that churches which take their missionary calling seriously are given an opportunity to learn anew that the unity of the Church is an essential part of the kerygma.

As long as churches live an introverted and self-centered life, and the responsibility for the evangelistic and missionary task is accepted only by a certain section of their membership, they may consider that the unity of the Church is a fine ideal which may belong to the *bene esse* of the Church, but which is not really necessary for the adequate fulfillment of its task. But when churches become permeated with a sense of missionary vocation, they must come to see that unity is of the *esse* of the Church. It is not simply that the missionary and evangelistic outreach of the churches requires a common strategy and a certain amount of co-operation. That is, of course, true, but it is only a small part of what is required for the adequate fulfillment of the task of witness. The real issue has to do with the *content* of the witness. The question arises whether it is possible to speak convincingly of the true meaning of

[6]Phil. 2:2, 4:2; Rom. 12:16, 15:5; 2 Cor. 13:11.

the Church of Christ without proclaiming that that Church is one and without manifesting that oneness in a concrete and visible manner. There is no doubt that the New Testament considers the oneness that is found in Christ, and which finds expression in the life of the primitive Church, as an essential part of the good news which it proclaims. That in Christ there had come into being a wholly new community, in which men and women of all tongues, races, classes, in which Jew and Gentile are made one, is part of the good news which the evangelists may announce. What Adolf von Harnack[7] tells us about the great importance of the message concerning "the new people" and "the third race" for the expansion of the Church in the first centuries is simply an illustration of the interdependence of mission and unity which we find in the high priestly prayer of John 17. There was a time when the Church was so manifestly one that many in the world came to believe in Jesus Christ because of the miracle of His power uniting those who had lived in complete separation from each other. This means that a missionary movement without concern for unity is in danger of defeating its own purpose. But it is no less true that an ecumenical movement without concern for missions contradicts its own nature. Such a movement might have some results in the field of unity, but these results would be superficial and probably not of a lasting character.

The witnessing task of the churches is so central that it is unthinkable that churches should meet together and enter into fellowship with each other without considering together what their common witness is and how they can best communicate that witness to the world. In this respect the "Faith and Order" movement set the good example. At its very first world conference in Lausanne in 1927 it did not only deal with the issues of interchurch relationships and church unity but also with "the Church's message to the world—the Gospel." During the long period of preparation for the conference, since 1910, this subject had not been on the agenda. In fact it was not until 1926 that it was added to the other points. But the report on this subject proved to be the only one of all section reports which found unanimous acceptance. Less than a year later at Jerusalem the International Missionary Council

[7] In *Die Mission und Ausbreitung des Christentums in den ersten drei Jahrhunderten*, Leipzig, 1906.

adopted this same report on the Christian message and said: "We are glad to make this our own."

It remains a remarkable fact that already in this early stage of the ecumenical movement it became clear that the churches were brought closer together when they considered their common message to the world than when they considered the internal problems of the family of churches. In the later stages this experience was confirmed. The Oxford Conference on Life and Work of 1937 produced more substantial results than the Stockholm Conference of 1925, precisely because it dealt much more resolutely with the content of the Christian witness and its relevance for the modern situation. And the World Council of Churches has found again and again that it is not in avoiding the difficult issues of the Church's witness but in facing them together that unity is advanced. Thus the seemingly impossible has become possible, namely, that churches which are still kept apart by important differences in faith and order have, nevertheless, been given a common word for the world both in matters of social and international life and in matters concerning the content of the Christian message. It would be folly to speak as if this common witness were sufficient and adequate, but it would be lack of gratitude not to recognize that it is a real gift of God to the churches in our generation that we have been enabled to speak out together on such vital issues as atomic tests and human rights, race relations and social justice. Our task is surely to do far more than we have done in preparing the day when, in their approach to the confused world of our day, the churches do not add to the confusion by offering contradictory messages, but bring one clear common message. It is necessary to emphasize that within such a message there must certainly be room for the varieties of the gifts of grace.

There is another important question that has to do with our common calling to witness. It is the question of the right relation of that part of the ecumenical movement which is concerned with missions to the other parts of the movement. We have seen that the world-wide dimension belongs to the nature of the witness. Every part of the ecumenical movement must be concerned with the missionary task.

The very word "ecumenical" requires the concern for the carrying of the news of God's great deeds to the four corners of the inhabited world. A unity which would not include common acceptance of the calling to world-wide witness would be a caricature of the unity meant in the New Testament. It would be a unity for the sake of the Church alone instead of the unity for the sake of God's work in the world.

It is, therefore, not because of organizational reasons that the ecumenical movement of the churches, embodied in the World Council of Churches, and the ecumenical movement of missions have been increasingly drawn together. There is a spiritual logic in the development of that close relationship. The World Council has been forced to become increasingly concerned about the missionary task of the Church. The International Missionary Council has been forced to become increasingly concerned about the life and nature of the Church. Both are concerned with the witness of the churches to the world. It becomes, therefore, increasingly difficult to find a meaningful line of demarcation between their respective fields of work.

Thus the two bodies are now considering a full integration. That integration should not only mean greater efficiency in organization or the avoiding of overlapping. It should mean a commitment to the spiritual integration and interpenetration of the various aspects of the total calling of the Church, which each has specially emphasized.

It should mean that, even more definitely than has been the case, the evangelistic and missionary dimension of the task of the Church becomes a central concern of the whole ecumenical movement. The common obligation of all churches to finish the unfinished task of the evangelization of the world must cease to be a concern of specialists and color the prayer, the life, and thought of the whole fellowship and of all its parts. And the question must be raised whether it is not the normal duty of each church to participate in the fulfillment of that obligation.

On the other hand, the missionary forces which have given much to the ecumenical movement will have to face the question whether the time has not come to draw even more far-reaching consequences from the existence of that movement than they have done so far. If it is true, as Bishop Azariah of India said in 1927 at the Lausanne

Conference, "The divisions of Christendom may be a source of weakness in Christian countries, but in non-Christian lands they are a sin and a scandal," then the mission bodies should be the vanguard of the movement for visible unity. And they can do this effectively only within a movement based on the churches, for it is the churches that are to be united. At the same time they can pave the way for such reality if they adopt a truly ecumenical strategy for their combined missionary operation. It is high time that the churches and the mission bodies together show the world that they face it with full awareness that unity is part of the missionary message and, therefore, also essential for missionary policy.

III

THE CALLING TO
SERVICE

St. Luke records that Jesus asked his disciples: "Which is the greater, one who sits at table, or one who serves? Is it not the one who sits at table?" (Lk. 22:27). This and other passages show us that the original meaning of *diakonein* is "to serve at table" (Lk. 4:39, 12:37, 17:8; Jn. 2:5, 9). And we learn at the same time that the old world considered service as undignified. A participant in one of Plato's dialogues says: "How can a man be happy, if he has to serve someone?"[1] It must, therefore, have been quite a shock to the disciples when Jesus added suddenly: "But I am among you as one who serves." The Lord, the promised Messiah, says really, think of me as a waiter.

The same contrast between the high claim of Jesus and the manner of his presence in the world is brought out even more sharply when the Lord is described as having come in "the form of a slave," as St. Paul does in Philippians 2.

The whole mission of Jesus can be described in that one word: service. The messianic King fulfills his function not in the manner of the Gentiles who "lord it" over their subjects but in the manner of the true servant, the center of whose life is the good of those whom he serves.

This had been foreshadowed in the Old Testament. In the

[1]Quoted in Kittel, *W.N.T.* II:81.

"servant hymns" of Isaiah it is said that the Servant of Jehovah "poured out his life for many" and thus "humbled himself."[2] There is clearly an echo of this prophecy in Mk. 10:45: "For the Son of man also came not to be served but to serve, and to give his life as a ransom for many." The tremendous paradox of the King who is servant, of the slave who is Lord of all is everywhere present in the New Testament as a marvelous mystery.

It is, in this connection, a very remarkable fact that in the fourth Gospel the story of the feet washing takes the place of the description of the last supper. For that shows how centrally important St. John must have considered the witness of Jesus' act of humility and diakonia. Now the chief significance of that act is once again that God in Christ takes the initiative in serving and that all of us, like Peter, react instinctively against such action. William Temple says: "We would gladly wash the feet of our Divine Lord; but He disconcertingly insists on washing ours, and bids us wash our neighbour's feet."[3] For that is the corollary: Because God comes to serve us, we are sent out among men as servants. "A slave is not greater than his master; nor is he who is sent greater than he who sent him" (Jn. 13:16). Our mission is a mission of diakonia, because we serve a servant. And we can only render the true service which men need if we have first accepted the service which God offers us Himself.

So our service is a service wholly qualified by the service of Christ. We are not to decide ourselves how men should be served. We are to follow Him in His service. "If any one serves me, he must follow me; and where I am, there shall my servant be also" (Jn. 12:26). We are inclined to think of service in purely moral terms. Quite early in the life of the post-Apostolic Church, service began to be considered as one of the good works.[4] But in the New Testament we have to do with something which goes much deeper and embraces the whole orientation of life. It is true that in the story of the feet washing Jesus speaks of His action as an "example" (Jn. 13:15), but that example is not merely a lesson in right behavior; it is, as the context shows, an invitation to accept a com-

[2] G. Adam Smith's translation of Is. 53.

[3] *Readings in St. John's Gospel*, Vol. 2, p. 214.

[4] W. Schneemelcher in *Das Diakonische Amt der Kirche*, 1953, p. 71.

plete revolution in one's life and to live the life of the new age inaugurated by Jesus. The kingdom has come in Him and with it a re-evaluation of all human values. In the kingdom the role of the servants is decisive, just as in this world is the role of the masters. This structural law of the kingdom must operate in the Church right now. And it can operate because the Lord who came to serve continued His work in and through the Church. By itself the Church is unable to operate this revolution of human relationships. But in so far as it is "in Christ" it is empowered to be a fellowship of men who serve the Lord, who serve each other, and who serve the world. The great passage of Philippians 2 concerning the self-emptying of Christ and His coming in the form of a slave begins, therefore: "Have this mind among yourselves, which you have in Christ Jesus," that is, which is given to you when you live in the communion created and sustained by Him. So the royal office of Christ finds its ecclesiological equivalent not in an ecclesiocracy—in which the Church rules the world—but in the diakonia attitude of the Church in the world.

It follows that the nature of our service must reflect the service which Christ has rendered. That means, above all, that service implies the solidarity of the servant with those whom he serves. Service is Christian if it is not service at a distance or service in which the gulf between the giver and the receiver remains unbridged, but is the service of solidarity between those who, in the last analysis, all live by the grace of the decisive and definitive service rendered by Christ. In giving His life on the cross, He has entered wholly into the existence of humanity with its sin and its suffering. "For because he himself has suffered and been tempted, he is able to help those who are tempted" (Heb. 2:18). The paradox of the Lord who is Servant comes to its climax when it must be said of Him: "He saved others; he cannot save himself" (Mt. 27:42). There is, then, nothing surprising in the fact that He speaks of service rendered to needy men as a service rendered to Himself (Mt. 25:40). For He has actually taken their place. He has carried out the prophecy of Isaiah 53 and borne the burden of humanity. The reconciliation between God and men is based on this supreme service by which He who knew no sin was made to be sin for our sakes (2 Cor. 5:21). That is the act of unlimited solidarity which must be the point of orientation for all Christian diakonia.

At this point we see most clearly the distinctiveness of Christian service. Diakonia is Christian if it is not merely a work of philanthropy or pity, but a true participation in suffering or need. The philanthropist and the sentimental observer may make real sacrifices, but they are not necessarily personally involved in the existence of those who need help. The Christian who seeks to serve as His Lord served must enter into the life of the needy. For that is the way God loves. Therefore, St. Paul says of the "agape," the love which reflects God's love: "If I give away all I have, and if I deliver my body to be burned, but have not agape, I gain nothing" (1 Cor. 13:3).

We must now ask how the calling to serve is fulfilled in the life of the Church. At this point we must distinguish between service in a more general sense and service in the more restricted and technical sense of help given to those in need. It is not always easy to discover in which sense the New Testament writers use diakonia, or service. The more general use is certainly predominant. All Christian life is service; all offices in the Church are ministries. When St. Paul says, "There are varieties of *diakoniai* [plural] but the same Lord" (1 Cor. 12:5), he refers obviously to all forms which the service of Christ may take in the life of the fellowship, and diakonia is, in this connection, practically synonymous with *charisma*, gift of grace. Similarly in Ephesians 4 "the work of ministry" (diakonia) is equivalent to the building up of the body of Christ. Thus the whole Church is called to participate in the comprehensive service. We have as much reason to speak of the general deaconhood of the believers as we have to speak of the general priesthood.

But this is not the only use of the term. Diakonia means, at the same time, a specific aspect of the calling of the Church: its responsibility for those who need specially to be helped: the poor, the sick, the prisoner, the homeless. Thus in Romans 12:7 diakonia is described as a specific charisma differing from the gifts of prophecy, of teaching, or of exhortation. Similarly in 1 Peter 4:11 diakonia is one of the ways in which God's varied grace expresses itself. It remains true that all are called to minister, but this does not exclude the specific calling which comes to some and which sets them apart in order to concentrate on the work of mercy and relief.[5]

This double use of the term also explains why it is so very difficult to define the nature of the task of the deacons in the New Testament. According to some passages they seem to be assistants to the *episkopos* (Phil. 1:1). But according to Acts 6 the Jerusalem church set seven men apart whose main task was "to serve at the tables," and it would seem that this terminology indicates that they were regarded as deacons.

The Church is a fellowship of mutual service. 1 Peter 4:10 says literally: "As each has received a gift of grace, serving each other as good stewards of God's varied grace." But there is a specific ministry to the needy. This is clearly illustrated by the fact that the collection for the saints in Jerusalem is called a diakonia. According to Acts 11:29, the disciples determined to send to the brethren who lived in Judea *eis diakonian*, that is, "for relief." St. Paul describes the collection in the same way (2 Cor. 9:1). He takes it for granted that the Corinthians know what he means when he speaks of the diakonia for the saints. And in several other passages the word diakonia becomes synonymous with "relief" (Rom. 15:25, 31; 2 Cor. 8:4).

This interchurch aid for the impoverished church in Jerusalem plays an astonishingly important role in the lifework of St. Paul. Knox comes to the conclusion that "for several years, we may believe, this offering was Paul's major preoccupation" and that "it had very important ecclesiastical, almost theological implications."[6] Cullmann considers that "when insoluble dogmatic and cultic differences split whole sections of the early Church in two camps, the apostles, while recognizing these differences in a frank and sincere manner, created nevertheless a bond of love, namely the collection for the poor of the Jerusalem church."[7] In other words, this financial campaign is vastly more than an act of philanthropy. It is a witness to the solidity of the bond between all who belong to Christ. It is the inevitable response to the One who, though He was rich, became poor for our sake and has bound all

[5]See H. D. Wendland in *Das Diakonische Amt der Kirche*, 1953, p. 449 ff.

[6]*The Early Church and the Coming Great Church*, p. 95.

[7]*Kirchenblatt für die Reformierte Schweiz*, Febr. 21, 1957.

His disciples together in the solidarity of gratitude. Dr. Knox could have left out the word "almost" when he said that the collection had "almost theological implications." The collection is a theological necessity because it is a necessary consequence of the Church's understanding of the gospel. There might be serious divergences between the Jerusalemites and the Pauline congregations; they might not see eye to eye about serious issues of the faith and of Christian life. But they still belonged to the one and only people of God, and so the divergences became an added reason for the ministry of relief. If it was, for the time being, impossible to arrive at full theological agreement, it was at least possible to show that the younger churches cared for the older and that, beyond all controversy, the law of the interdependence of the body was still operative.

For diakonia creates and nourishes koinonia. St. Paul speaks in 2 Corinthians 8:4 of the *koinonia tes diakonias*—the fellowship which is manifested in and fortified by the service rendered to each other by the churches. As the churches actually live as members of the body in which the suffering of one member means the suffering of all the body, they are participating in the work of the ministry, the building up of the body of Christ (Eph. 4:12).

So far we have mainly spoken of the service which members of the Christian fellowship render to each other. But is that the whole story? The Christian Church has often given the impression that it is only a mutual aid society and that it is exclusively occupied with the building up of its own life. But the New Testament speaks differently. It speaks of the Lord who came to minister and to give His life as a ransom for *many*—and that means for the whole of humanity. And in the great scene of the last judgment this King declares that any act of mercy done to the least of His brethren is in fact an act of mercy to the King Himself.

There are those who interpret this last passage as if it meant that Jesus only recognizes the service rendered to His disciples. It is true that there are other passages in the Gospels in which the act of mercy which Jesus praises is one for His disciples (Mt. 10:42). But there is no reason to interpret Matthew 25 in the light of those passages. On the contrary. For in this chapter there is nothing to indicate that the hungry or thirsty are disciples of Christ. In the Gospels, as in the Old Testament, the Word "brethren" is often used for all members of the Jewish people and by no means only for the small community of the disciples. The "least" are like the "little ones" in Luke 17:2 and in Matthew 18:10 the "poor" to whom the kingdom of heaven is promised. They are the needy ones, the humiliated and downtrodden, the ones whom (as is implied in Mt. 18:10) we naturally despise, but who are precisely for that reason specially protected by God.[8] According to the Magnificat, the coming of the Messiah means that the hungry are filled with good things. And this prophecy is fulfilled when Jesus preaches good news to the poor and when He feeds the multitudes.

The Jesus who tells us that the neighbor is not merely the fellow countryman but anyone with whom life brings us in contact, be he Samaritan or Jew, and who asks us to love our enemies because the Father sends rain on the just and the unjust does certainly not say to us: "As you minister to a member of my church, you minister to me," but rather: "As you minister to one in whom you find it very hard to recognize one of my brethren, you render service to me, for all belong to me and I have come especially to seek the lost."

So Karl Barth's words are true: The least of Jesus' brethren "are in an exemplary way the world, for which he died and rose again, with which he has identified himself to the highest degree and with which he has declared himself to be in solidarity."[9] And Matthew 25 remains indeed "the Magna Charta of Christian Humanism and of Christian politics."[10]

St. Paul, whose main emphasis is, as we have seen, on the ministry to the saints in Jerusalem, does not forget this universal dimension of diakonia. He quotes the book of Proverbs: "If your enemy is hungry, feed him; if he is thirsty, give him drink" (Rom. 12:20). And to the Galatians he writes: "So then, as we have opportunity, let us do good to all men, and especially to those who are of the household of faith" (Gal. 6:10).

There is, then, an external as well as an internal diakonia. The

[8]See W. G. Kümmel, *Verheissung und Erfüllung*, Basel, 1945, pp. 54–56.

[9]*Kirchliche Dogmatik* III:2:611. *Cf. K.D.* IV: 2:188–89.

[10]Ibidem, p. 612.

internal one is the natural form of existence of a community bound together by their common service to the Servant of the Lord. But the external diakonia is the necessary consequence of the fact that the service of the divine Servant was aimed at the many and that His followers are called to share in His act of humiliation and reconciliation.

Thus whenever the Church of Christ has been truly awake, it has not only maintained its ministry to its own members but gone out into the world in order to meet the needs of men.

The early Christians knew that they were not merely called to serve each other but all who were in need. The biographer of St. Cyprian tells us how St. Cyprian organized a relief operation at the time of the plague in Carthago and adds simply: "They did good to all and not merely to the family of the faithful."[11] Eusebius describes a similar Christian enterprise: "Others [Christians] gathered in the whole city those who suffered from hunger and distributed bread to all. As this became known, people praised the God of the Christians and admitted that they [the Christians] alone were truly pious and God-fearing, because they proved it by their deeds."[12] And we have this remarkable testimony from the last of the pagan emperors, Julian: "These godless Galileans do not only feed their own poor, but even ours."[13]

In the New Testament the ministry to the needy is, first of all, a ministry from person to person. There is little explicit reference to that other form of service which consists in the struggle against social injustice or in the transformation of the social structure. But that does not mean that there is no biblical basis at all for the service of which the object is not a single person but society as a whole.

For both the "law" and the "prophets" had spoken strong and clear words about the issues of justice and injustice in society. The Deuteronomic literature is especially insistent in its rejection of the various forms of social exploitation and in its demand for economic solidarity. The great prophets condemn in no uncertain terms the wrongs of the rich and proclaim that God's will for His

[11]Harnack, *Mission and Ausbreitung*, p. 179.

[12]Ibidem.

[13]Loc. cit., p. 170.

people is that they shall reflect the divine righteousness in a righteous social order. Now Jesus does not abolish the law and the prophets but He fulfills them (Mt. 5:17). The claims which God had made under the old covenant are not abrogated. They are sharpened in Jesus' proclamation concerning the kingdom. They are realized in the coming of the Messiah Himself. This becomes clear in Jesus' attitude to the poor, the underprivileged, the outcasts from society. It finds expression in His own explanation of His mission when, in the synagogue at Nazareth, He quotes Isaiah 61, saying: "He has sent me to proclaim release to the captives and recovering of sight to the blind, to set at liberty those who are oppressed" (Lk. 4:18), or when, in answer to John the Baptist, He quotes the same chapter, saying: "The poor have good news preached to them" (Mt. 11:5). For it would be wrong to interpret these passages only in a "spiritual" and not at the same time in a "social" sense. The words of the Magnificat show that we have not merely to do with spiritual attitudes but also with objective situations: "He has put down the mighty from their thrones, and exalted those of low degree; he has filled the hungry with good things, and the rich he has sent empty away" (Lk. 1:52-53).

For the New Testament Church it was out of the question to perform the wider ministry of the struggle against injustice in society. Its belief that the kingdom would come very soon made the concern with society seem unnecessary. At the same time the issues of society as such did not become living existential issues for them. For they lived in a centralized authoritarian state in which they could not possibly exert a direct influence on legislation or public action with regard to social conditions. Their strength was precisely that they dealt with the concrete issues within their own community, such as those of the family or of the relations between masters and slaves.

But most Christians today live in a different situation. If we are to be true to our calling, we have to deal with the real issues with which we are confronted in the light of the whole biblical proclamation. We are confronted with the general economic and political, as well as with the personal, aspects of hunger, sickness, homelessness, exploitation, injustice. Christian obedience for us means, therefore, both the personal service to the needy and the tackling of the social problems in their wider economic and political aspects. We act as priests and levites on the road from Jerusalem to Jericho not only if we do not seize the opportunity to give direct help to the individual victim of society but also if we do not seize the opportunity to help the masses of individual victims of social disorder, and in all possible ways, including social and political action.

We must, then, also engage in that wider service which includes participation and pioneering in the elaboration of social legislation and in national or international actions to combat social need and social injustice. It is true that this form of service has its peculiar spiritual dangers. The precious element of concern of persons to persons and of true identification with the needy is easily lost in welfare schemes and comprehensive plans of technical assistance. But the existence of these dangers is not a sufficient reason for refusing to help in such a way that the needs of the masses are really met. We must not, for fear of losing sight of the human person, let millions of human persons live in a misery which is likely to kill all truly personal life. On the other hand, our Christian task in the era of the welfare state and of international schemes of assistance is to make certain that the welfare state or the international society do not become the only instruments of service, and to maintain, therefore, as large a volume of specifically Christian person-centered diakonia as we possibly can. At the same time we must share in the difficult task to save the large secular agencies from becoming impersonal machineries. This means that we must encourage Christian laymen to enter into the service of those bodies.

There is yet another question which is vitally important for a right understanding of the place of diakonia in the Christian Church: Is the true raison d'être of diakonia to be found in its relation to evangelism? Or does it stand on its own feet? Is Christian service to be evaluated in terms of its effectiveness in bringing men to a knowledge and acceptance of the gospel or in terms of its ability to meet human need? In the light of what we have said about the source and dynamic of service in the New Testament sense, the answer is clear. Diakonia does not need any other justification than that which it has in the life and the death of Christ. This was the form of His existence, His way of life. This was the road on which He asked His disciples to follow Him. Diakonia has its own original dignity. It is a direct manifestation of the nature and calling of the Church. The criteria in the light of which Christian service is to be judged are those of diakonia itself, whether it is truly a response of gratitude for the service of Christ, whether it springs from disinterested love for the needy, whether it seeks to bridge the gulf between the giver and the receiver.

The offer of service must, therefore, never be made dependent on the fulfillment of conditions by the receiver. He is worthy of service simply because he is one of those with whom Christ identified Himself, for whom He suffered and died. It is precisely this service without calculation and without counting on any return which is blessed by the King in the parable of the last judgment (Mt. 25).

Unfortunately the Christian churches have given, and are often giving, the impression that diakonia is in fact an auxiliary activity, an instrument for their evangelistic or missionary expansion. A good deal of the great misunderstanding between the Church and the modern world has arisen precisely at this point. The world finds it hard to believe that Christians can render truly disinterested service and have a concern about man as man and not merely as potential church members.

Does this mean that marturia and diakonia, the witness and the service of the Church, are completely unrelated? Certainly not. All aspects of the one calling are interdependent. By serving, the Church manifests the love of Christ for men. But this manifestation takes a specific form, the form of deeds. And this manifestation through what has been called "the pantomime of faith"[14] has its own independent function and significance.

This does not mean that the real meaning of Christian service is necessarily understood by those to whom it is rendered. It is an illusion to think that our service can be made so transparent that it will by itself lead those whom we serve to a confrontation with Jesus Christ. There is so much ambiguity in our actions that they cannot take the place of the explicit and spoken witness to the gospel. That is also why we must never use diakonia as an excuse for not preaching the gospel in situations where we may expect that our witness in words will be understood.

Since diakonia and marturia are closely related as manifestations of one and the same love of God which seeks men, they should not

[14]Title of an article by H. Hoekendijk in *Wending*.

be separated unless there are strong reasons to do so. Where the Church is alive and can operate in full freedom, the two will be found together. But it happens that situations arise in which the Church is forced to restrict itself to the proclamation of the Word. Again it is today not infrequent that, either because of government regulations or because of a deep mistrust of the Church, the only possibility of action lies in silent service. Now it is easy to see that where the ministry to the needy is impossible, the Church has the duty to continue to preach the gospel. Is the same true of diakonia? It is. We are called to minister to men in need even if there is no reason to hope that our ministry will now or later create opportunities for an explicit witness.

In this matter of the relation of diakonia and marturia, we are constantly faced with two temptations: the temptation to render only such service as will provide a point of contact for, or introduction to the evangelistic encounter or the temptation to provide only a silent ministry where more, namely the ministry together with the announcement of the good news, is required.

We must, therefore, learn to distinguish between different situations: those into which we enter with no other purpose than to serve men in their need without even asking ourselves whether this ministry will open doors for evangelistic action and those in which the ministry has not only a value in itself but also a further value in preparing the way for evangelism. And we must be ready to accept these two types of situations as of equal importance for our Christian task.

We must be willing to render disinterested service in a milieu of workers in which we may hope that new relations of confidence can slowly be established so that someday we may speak to them about the Christian faith. Diakonia can create the conditions for a new conversation. Thus it could be said of the priest-workers in France that "the word which the church addresses to the world of the workers is the existence of the priest-workers."[15] Bonhoeffer speaks in this connection of the Christian task to be concerned with the "penultimate," that is, the conditions of true human existence before we concern ourselves with the "ultimate," that is, the confrontation with the gospel.[16] In those situations our diakonia has a

[15]André Collange, quoted in Le Monde, June 13, 1957.
[16]Bonhoeffer, Ethik, München, 1949, p. 86.

twofold meaning, a meaning in itself and a meaning as the preparing of the way for the gospel. We do not, then, serve simply in order to win souls. We serve because we are followers of the great Servant. But we know that the supreme service consists in bringing people to the Servant Himself.

But we must be equally willing to minister to human need in a milieu where we cannot expect that our ministry will pave the way for evangelism. For men who do not or cannot listen to the gospel remain creatures of God and brothers for whom Christ died.

We must, of course, never seek to hide the reasons why we are engaged in the work of diakonia and always be ready to give an account of our faith when we are asked to do so. We should have a bad conscience if we do not seize a clear opportunity, when it is given to us, to announce the gospel. But we should not have a bad conscience if we have to wait a long time for such an opportunity, or even if it never comes.

What does this mean for the ecumenical movement? It means these three things:

1) The ecumenical movement should keep prominently before the churches the obligation to serve each other and should provide channels for such interchurch service.

If it belongs to the very nature of the Church that its several parts serve each other, interchurch aid cannot be conceived as a temporary task of the ecumenical movement to be undertaken only in times of crisis. In the life of the churches sharing must not be the abnormal but rather the normal practice. The World Council of Churches became involved in the work of reconstruction and interchurch aid because of the emergency situation created by the second World War, but as it sought to meet the most crying needs of the churches, it discovered that it had, in fact, engaged in a task which was so essential for the life of the whole fellowship that it could not possibly discontinue it. Interchurch aid is essential because it proves, in the most concrete way, that the churches really intend to stay together, as they promised each other in Amsterdam in 1948. Interchurch service means that the churches share their resources in all realms. Financial aid in emergency situations or in situations where churches cannot, for the time being, meet their own financial needs is important. But it is only a part of the total task. There is the help through fraternal workers which, by bringing the personal element into the relationships, can give diakonia a deeper meaning. There is the spiritual and moral backing given to churches which are in the midst of a struggle for their freedom.

Interchurch service is not a monopoly of the stronger and the larger churches. Every church, however weak, is called to participate in it. It is one of the most encouraging developments of recent years that so many churches, including churches which had so far not been giving churches, have begun to participate in the ecumenical ministry of service. For every church has something to give which other churches need. And every church has something to receive from other churches. Interchurch aid is characterized by the combination of generosity in giving and humility in receiving.

If diakonia is to have its full effect in the relations of the churches, it is of special importance that aid not be restricted to churches of the same confessional family. Each such family has, of course, a special responsibility for its own members. But if the churches are to live up to their common calling, they must demonstrate that they consider churches of other confessions as part of the body within which the principle of solidarity operates, so that the suffering of one is the suffering of all. Following the example of St. Paul, churches should help each other, not in spite of disagreement but because of disagreement, for giving creates that bond of love on the basis of which disagreement may be overcome.

2) The ecumenical movement must help the churches to be servant churches in the society in which they live.

The conviction that the Church is called to serve is not born in our time. But that conviction came with new force and in a new manner to the generation of men to whom we owe the creation of the ecumenical movement. The Stockholm Conference of 1925 could not yet give much substantial guidance to the churches on their role in society, but it did two important things. The first was to make it clear that the service of the churches was not only to be thought of in terms of individual service to the needy but also in terms of proclaiming the implications of the gospel of justice and love to the life of society. The second thing was to admit that the churches had failed to perform this ministry of being watchmen to the nations and of speaking prophetically to the peoples.

Thus a new spiritual process was started. Through the series of further ecumenical conferences since Stockholm, the nature of the Church's task in society was clarified, and a substantial consensus concerning the meaning of the "responsible society" was achieved. This basic consensus is one of the most hopeful results of ecumenical work in recent decades.[17]

But it is one thing to have arrived at such agreement in ecumenical gatherings; it is another to get churches and church members to live up to the principles on which their representatives have agreed. So far, few churches have made sufficient efforts to mobilize Christian laymen for the purpose of working out concretely what consequences they should draw from the results of ecumenical study in this field. It is, however, clear that just as we owe it largely to the full participation of laymen in the international study that our conclusions were not irrelevant, so the churches will only be able to speak concretely on social affairs if they ask their laymen to give time and energy for this purpose. Precisely because we know so much better that the Church has a prophetic task in society, we are in greater spiritual danger if that task is not actually undertaken in the concrete circumstances of each church, of each local congregation.

3) The ecumenical movement must help the churches see their service in the perspective of the total needs of mankind, and act for the churches in relation to needs which can be met only by the churches acting together.

Interchurch service and service in the immediate environment are not enough. In a world in which men, goods, and ideas travel along all roads in all directions and in which men fall "among robbers" by the millions, the good Samaritan is called upon to be a neighbor to men in need everywhere. The universal Lord is a universal Servant and His Church must express in its diakonia, as well as in its marturia, that He came for all men. Thus each church, however small and however poor, is to participate in the world-wide service to men in need.

The ecumenical service to refugees, which has been responsible for the settling of over 200,000 refugees in new homes, exemplifies this dimension of diakonia. It has its interchurch aid aspects, for

[17]See the brochure, *Statements of the W.C.C. on Social Questions.*

many refugees are Christians cut off from their churches, and for them we have a special responsibility. But it also has its wider aspects, for we are called upon to help large numbers of refugees who are outside the Christian fold. The refugee problem is, of course, a world problem which can be solved only by the co-operation of churches in many parts of the world. But the refugee service shows, at the same time, the specific functions of the churches in meeting human need. For the refugee is a person whose material need, great as it is, is overshadowed by his spiritual problem of being uprooted and finding new roots. To help him effectively is to help him pastorally.

The type of service which the ecumenical movement is called upon to render in relation to the great social needs of our time is also illustrated by the study of "the common Christian responsibility for areas of rapid social change." That is not a study in the sense of pure research, but an attempt to help the churches in the areas concerned find out how they can accomplish their mission in preindustrial societies which are disrupted and transformed by the invasion of the modern industrial, technical, and urban civilization. The churches have a very specific responsibility because this transformation creates spiritual and moral problems which cannot be solved at the political level. They are called upon to complement, by a Christian social service mainly concerned with human beings and their relations to each other, the social and economic measures of governments which, in the nature of the case, are mainly concerned with the production of goods. The task can be accomplished only ecumenically, for the size of the problem is such that all resources must be pooled.

Thus many great needs in our modern world can be met only by church action on the international level. It has proved possible to arrive at widespread spontaneous collaboration between the churches with regard to great emergencies such as floods, earthquakes, and famine. But why should such general co-operation be confined to times of sudden emergency and not also take place with regard to *continuing* human needs? It would seem that the time has come for the Christian churches to create more permanent international and interconfessional forms of co-operation in the field of diakonia. The possibilities with regard to education, health, and social development are enormous. It is time to complement the various forms of international technical assistance to nations which need such service by projects of international Christian assistance. Such international projects would have the added advantage that they would be less liable to become suspect as being in the interests of any particular nation.

Thus the calling of the churches to serve has now a new global dimension. We must increasingly create a type of diakonia which is world-wide in its outreach, its strategy, its spirit. This common service may become an increasingly powerful factor in the growth of Christian unity. That will not happen automatically. It will happen only if the service is undertaken as a welcome opportunity to show that the Lord who became Servant intends us to serve together.

IV

THE CALLING TO
FELLOWSHIP IN CHRIST

————◆————

THE CHURCH is not only called to witness and to serve but also to exemplify what the new life means for the relationships in which Christians live. These relationships are, in the nature of the case, not merely the relationships between men. The New Testament can no more conceive of human relations apart from the relation to God in Christ than it can conceive of a relation to God isolated from the relation of fellow men. That is why we must use as the title of this chapter: The calling to fellowship in Christ (cf. 1 Cor. 1:9). This two-dimensioned character of the Christian life is most strikingly expressed in the word: koinonia. That word is one of the key words of the New Testament. In one of the earliest descriptions of the life of the Church it appears as a main characteristic of that life (Acts 2:42). It plays a central role in the epistles of St. Paul and also in the first epistle of St. John. The richness of its meaning is indicated by the fact that the Revised Standard Version uses four different words to translate it: fellowship, communion, participation, and contribution. We need not enter into a discussion of the linguistic problems connected with the interpretation of its basic meaning.[1] The recent studies on the subject arrive at convergent

[1]Davies, *Members One of Another*, London, 1958.
Hauck, article "Koinonia" in *Kittel Wörterbuch III.*
Thornton, *The Common Life in the Body of Christ,* 1942.
A. Raymond George, *Communion with God in the New Testament,* London, 1953.

conclusions. For our purpose the following points are specially important.

The basic meaning of the word is that men share with each other a common possession. This meaning is, however, developed in three directions: the first is "having a share or participation"; the second, "giving a share or contribution"; the third, "fellowship."[2] It is sometimes difficult to know which is the precise meaning of the word in a specific context. But it is clear that when the word is used as a description of the life of the Church, it includes always the vertical dimension of the relation to God as well as the horizontal dimension of relations between men. To this extent, the translation "fellowship" is misleading. For fellowship may mean, of course, a friendly relation between men without any particular horizontal or even spiritual dimension. Thus when we read in Acts 2:42 that at the very beginning of their common life the Christians "devoted themselves to the apostles' teaching and fellowship [koinonia], to the breaking of bread and the prayers," we might think that "fellowship" just refers to their happy social relationships or to their experiment in sharing their possessions. But if we watch the total context and remember that our passage is preceded by Peter's announcement of the gift of the Holy Spirit (verse 38), then it becomes clear that here as elsewhere koinonia is the common participation in the divine gifts and promises.[3]

The vertical and the horizontal dimensions are most often described as aspects of one and the same reality.

In 1 John 1:2 the fellowship "with us" that is between the apostle and the recipients of his letter is the common fellowship "with the Father and with His Son Jesus Christ." In Romans 15:26 the word koinonia is used for the contribution to the poor of Jerusalem, but this matter of human charity is explained in the next verse as a consequence of a common sharing (koinonein) in the spiritual blessings, that is, in the blessings given by the Holy Spirit.

The ground of the fellowship is the work of Christ. Christians are not called into a vague, undefined fellowship. God calls them "into the fellowship of His Son, Jesus Christ our Lord" (1 Cor. 1:9); they are to participate in the specific history, the act of salvation

[2]A. Raymond George, op. cit., p. 238.

[3]See Raymond George, op. cit., p. 131 ff.

which God has initiated and accomplished in the sending of His Son. They are called to koinonia in the Spirit (Phil. 2:1), that is, to participate, to be involved in the life-giving activity of the Holy Spirit. When, in the words of blessing, the grace of the Lord Jesus Christ and the love of God are followed by "the koinonia of the Holy Spirit" (2 Cor. 13:14), the meaning is probably again, in the first place, the participation in the Holy Spirit, but it is inevitable that the kindred meaning of fellowship is also included.

Koinonia is, therefore, the way of life, the relationship with God and man which are characteristic of the community of those who are the objects of God's saving work in Christ. They are called into the koinonia of Jesus Christ by the God who is faithful (1 Cor. 1:9) and who constantly recreates and strengthens the koinonia.

But what does this mean for the internal life of the Christian community? It means that their life is a constant sharing with each other. Canon Warren puts it thus: "Here is the secret of the commonwealth of Christians. All are equally involved, all have committed themselves to God in trust, all have a share in a common responsibility, all recognise that they belong together, that if one member suffers all suffer, all have a liability for each. The Christian adventure as the New Testament presents it is intended to be an adventure in partnership."[4] Sharing embraces all aspects of life. There is sharing in suffering (2 Cor. 1:7, Heb. 10:33) but also in consolation (2 Cor. 1:7). There is sharing in tribulation and endurance but also in (the expectation of) the kingdom (Rev. 1:9). But the strongest proof of the comprehensiveness of the sharing is surely the fact that St. Paul uses the word *koinonia* not only when he seeks to explain the true meaning of the holy communion but also when he describes the significance of the collection for the poor in Jerusalem. In 1 Corinthians 10:16 we read: "The cup of blessing which we bless, is it not koinonia in [of] the blood of Christ? The bread which we break, is it not koinonia in [of] the body of Christ?" And in Romans 15:26 we read: "For Macedonia and Achaia have been pleased to make some koinonia [contribution] for the poor among the saints at Jerusalem." Now the use of the same word for two apparently very different realities cannot be explained by the fact that a very general expression happens to fit two quite different contexts, so that more or less accidentally

[4]Max Warren, *Partnership*, London, 1956, p. 52.

the heart of the central Christian mystery of union with Christ and the very practical business of a relief campaign for Jerusalem are described in the same way. For in both Romans 15 and in 2 Corinthians 8 and 9,[5] St. Paul places the collection for the poor in the framework of the sharing which flows from God's gifts to us in Christ. The collection was "proof positive of the actuality of the koinonia, that Jew and Gentile were one in Christ."[6] The communion and the relief action have in common that they are both manifestations of the shared life and the life of sharing.

The Christian Church is then characterized by a spiritual economy in which there are no frontiers, no restrictions on free trade. The gifts of grace are given for the good of all (1 Cor. 12:7); they are not to be capitalized or stored away. The description of the give and take, of the variety working toward harmony, of the mutual interdependence in the body of Christ which we have in 1 Corinthians 12 is (in spite of the fact that the word is not used there) the great charter of koinonia.

The description which the Acts of the Apostles and the epistles of St. Paul give us of the life of the earliest Christian churches show that the most concentrated expressions of koinonia are the holy communion and the common prayers of intercession.

The holy communion constitutes, proclaims, and realizes the koinonia of the believers with Christ and of the believers with each other.

It *constitutes* the fellowship because it "re-present-s," that is, it makes present and contemporary the central historic event of the crucifixion, through which the broken fellowship between God and man and, therefore, also between men themselves is restored. Just as Israel was constituted as the people of God by the covenant of the Sinai, so the new people of God is constituted by the covenant of Golgotha. This covenant is renewed and the new people, as it were, reconstituted when the believers receive the covenant pledge, that is, the bread and wine.

At the same time, the holy communion *proclaims* the communion with Christ and between the faithful themselves in that it reveals, in the most concrete manner, what koinonia really means.

[5]See also Phil. 4:14-19.

[6]J. G. Davies, *Members One of Another*, London, 1958, p. 32.

Here it becomes abundantly clear that the ground of koinonia is not the good will of man but the act of God in sending His Son. The "happened-ness" (as von Hügel called it), which is the center of the Christian faith, finds expression in the action of eating and drinking. The reality of the fellowship thus created finds expression in the meal at which, as in a true family, all eat from one and the same loaf and drink from one and the same cup.

The holy communion *realizes* the communion since Christ Himself acts in and through it. He has given Himself once for all in His death on the cross, but this becomes actualized in the eucharist. He had died "to gather into one the scattered children of God" (Jn. 11:52). Now these children of God are in fact gathered into one, into the unity of the one body. For as they "all partake of the same loaf" the "many are one body" (1 Cor. 10:17). St. Augustine said: "Since then you are the body of Christ and his members, it is your mystery that is placed on the Lord's table; it is your mystery that you receive" and this can be rephrased: "Since you are the koinonia of Christ, it is your mystery that is placed on the Lord's table, it is your mystery that you receive."[7]

Similarly the fellowship in Christ expresses itself in constant intercession for all members of the family of God. The prayers have nearly always a corporate character in that they are prayers of the whole fellowship and their theme is the life of the whole church. The Ephesians are exhorted to pray at all times in the Spirit . . . making supplications for all the saints, that is, for the whole body of Christians (Eph. 6:18). The prayer contained in the third chapter of that letter, that the Ephesians may comprehend the fullness of Christ's love, includes also "all the saints" (Eph. 3:18). Similarly the intercession of the Spirit, of which Romans 8:27 speaks, is an intercession "for the saints." St. Paul asks again and again for the prayers of the faithful for his own ministry (Rom. 15:30, Col. 4:3, 1 Thess. 5:25, 2 Thess. 3:1). There can be no koinonia without intercession.

Koinonia belongs, then, to the very essence of the Church. But does that mean that it must always have priority? Or are there situations in which, for the sake of truth, the demands of fellowship must give way? For the New Testament writers, and particu-

[7]Thus rephrased in J. G. Davies, op. cit., p. 22.

larly for St. Paul, this was not merely a theoretical question but a grave existential issue.

The classical New Testament passage which deals with the tension between uncompromising loyalty to the revealed truth and the loyalty to the God-given and Christ-centered fellowship of the one Church is the second chapter of the epistle to the Galatians. It has been interpreted in very divergent ways. But it would seem that recent studies on the subject lead to a consensus on some fundamental points.

Thus it seems clear that the account which St. Paul gives in this chapter of the decisive encounter between Pauline- and Jerusalem-centered Christianity is more realistic than the much less dramatic and "edited" account of this encounter in the Acts of the Apostles (Chapter 15). Many other passages in the New Testament show that St. Paul has not exaggerated the seriousness of the conflict. The young Christian Church consisted at that time of two sectors, or movements, each with its own theology and ethos. There were the Christian congregations which had received the gospel directly from Jerusalem and there were the congregations which had been created by the missionary work of St. Paul. The differences in outlook were so great that it was a very real problem how these two types of Christianity could be held together. In these circumstances St. Paul's visit to the Jerusalem leaders became of decisive importance.

St. Paul tells us that the first result of the visit was that an agreement was worked out which we would call today a "comity" agreement. The Jerusalem church would work among the Jews; St. Paul and his collaborators would work among the Gentiles. In this way the fellowship (koinonia) between the two sectors of the Church was recognized and re-established. Unfortunately the agreement proved in some ways impracticable because there were so many congregations where Jews and Gentiles were found together. Thus it was inevitable that further conflicts should arise and the first of these conflicts took place at Antioch. St. Paul had to oppose St. Peter publicly, for although St. Peter had at first accepted the agreement, he came under the influence of the more radical Jerusalem representatives and refused to have fellowship with the Gentile Christians.

This chapter has often been used to show that for St. Paul

the one and only concern was the concern for the purity of the message with which he was entrusted and that the claims of truths come before the claims of fellowship. Now this interpretation is true as far as it goes, but it does not go far enough. It is a fact that here, as elsewhere, we see St. Paul taking his stand on the truth of the gospel which had been revealed to him and that he did not hesitate to speak out openly against those who had greater "ecclesiastical" authority than he had when the truth of that gospel was at stake. But it is also true that this chapter does not only deal with complete devotion to the truth of God but, at the same time, with the struggle to maintain Christian koinonia in nearly impossible circumstances.[8] For why does St. Paul go to Jerusalem at all? He writes: "I laid before them the Gospel which I preach among the Gentiles, lest somehow I should be running or had run in vain?" (verse 2.) Why in vain? Did that gospel not have its justification in the fact that it had been revealed to St. Paul and that it had brought so many Gentiles to Christ? St. Paul must mean that his work would have been in vain if it had to be considered as a special or separatist gospel, unrelated to the gospel preached by the original community of Jerusalem. For the oneness of the new people belonged to the content of the gospel, and to contradict that oneness by separate existence would be to deny the gospel itself.

Thus the giving of the right hand of koinonia means vastly more than an act of politeness when, after difficult negotiations, a mutually acceptable agreement is worked out. This koinonia means no less than that the great reality of the oneness of God's people is reaffirmed, and this is to find its concrete manifestation in the collection for the poor in Jerusalem. And in spite of the conflict in Antioch and later conflicts, that koinonia is maintained.

So the story of the early Church is at the same time a story about loyalty to truth and about adherence to the basic fellowship. It is a dialectical story which should warn us against a defense of truth without concern for fellowship, as well as against an idolizing of fellowship without taking the question of truth seriously. Koinonia

[8]See Knox, *The Early Church and the Coming Great Church*, New York, 1955, p. 40.
Brandon, *The Fall of Jerusalem and the Christian Church*, London, 1951, pp. 18–19.
Cullman, *Peter: Disciple, Apostle, Martyr*, London, 1953, p. 49 ff.
Oepke, *Das neue Gottesvolk*, Gütersloh, 1950, pp. 183–88.

implies looking "to the interests of others" (Phil. 2:4). What that means is clearly illustrated by St. Paul's attitude during his last visit to Jerusalem (Acts 21:17 ff). The situation between him and the Jerusalem community was still full of tension. Between the Jewish Christians "all zealous for the law" (Acts 21:20) and the man who proclaimed that "neither circumcision counts for anything, nor uncircumcision" (Gal. 6:15), a truly "ecumenical" understanding could not easily be established. St. Paul even wonders whether the gift from the Gentile Christians for the poor in Jerusalem will be acceptable (Rom. 15:31). And when he arrives he is immediately faced with a difficult decision. St. James, the leader of the Jerusalem church, asks St. Paul to prove his loyalty to the Jewish law by participating in Jewish rites, including a vow and a purification ceremony. If St. Paul accepts, there is the danger that his Gentile Christian congregations may misunderstand him and take his action as a denial of the freedom of Christians from the law. If he does not accept, the unity of the people of God will be broken and that goes against the very raison d'être of that people and can have disastrous spiritual consequences for the missionary witness. St. Paul decides to accept. He had written that love does not insist on its own way (1 Cor. 13:5) and now he proves it. Faced with a real dilemma and in the name of the very freedom which Christ has given him, he becomes again a Jew to the Jews in order to maintain the koinonia which he considers essential in and for the people of God and its calling in the world.

St. Paul's answer to the problem of divergent convictions in the Church is, therefore: Do not turn your back upon those whose convictions differ from yours; confront them with the truth which you have received from God; seek to arrive at a real agreement; manifest in concrete acts of service your concern for them; make such sacrifices as you can make without going against your conscience; seek to maintain the fellowship which is essential if the church is to manifest the fullness of Christ's reconciling work.

What does this mean for the ecumenical movement? Hebrews 3:1 speaks of "brethren, who share in a heavenly call." The New Testament teaching about koinonia means for us, in the first place, that the churches must recognize that their sister churches in the movement have received that same call and are, therefore, partners in obedience. In the most controversial section of the Toronto statement on "The Church, the Churches and the World Council of Churches," which discusses the question of how far the churches in the Council recognize each other as churches in the true and full sense of the word, we find these simple words: "They [the churches which are members of the World Council] recognize one another as serving the one Lord." This is a statement of tremendous significance if it is taken seriously. For everything else follows from that. Where there is a clear acknowledgment of the common calling, the forces of *koinonia* must begin to operate in spite of all obstacles.

In which ways do they operate?

First of all, by creating in each church that sense of responsibility for and solidarity with the other churches, which is expressed in St. Paul's phrase, "the care of all the churches" (2 Cor. 11:28). What St. Paul meant by that phrase is explained in 1 Corinthians 12:25–26 where he says that "the various members [of the body] should have a common concern for one another" so that "if one member suffers all the members share its suffering; if one member is honoured all the members share its honour."[9] In other words, the Christian way of caring for the churches is not simply to be generally interested in them or even to exercise philanthropy toward them, but to be personally involved in their weakness and strength, in their sufferings and joys. St. Paul makes it clear that this concern is not to be merely the concern of men whose lifework has ecumenical dimensions, but the concern of all members. To keep oneself informed about the life of the whole Church of God, to know about the persecutions to which fellow Christians are subjected, about the witness given by churches under totalitarian regimes, about the progress of missions, about the movements of renewal in different churches is, therefore, not to indulge in an ecumenical "hobby," but to accomplish a simple Christian duty.

For thus only can we give meaning to that commandment and privilege of which the New Testament speaks so often: to pray for each other. In the prayers of all the churches, prayers for the Church Universal are included. Such prayers can, however, remain a pure abstraction, for reference to the Church Universal without

[9] Translation, Moffatt.

giving that concept any definite content leaves our prayers totally vague. It is only when we begin to pray specifically for those churches, those groups, those individuals about whose needs we really know something that ecumenical intercession becomes relevant. We are today in the privileged condition that we can know a great deal about the struggles of other churches. So we should learn to read our information services or church papers as helps to meaningful intercession.

Churches which recognize one another as serving the one Lord will, furthermore, want to enter into serious conversation with one another. They will want to do so, first of all, to receive from other churches the spiritual gifts which have been given to the latter "for the common good." It is a strange thing that we still hear so much about the gifts which the various church families desire to bestow upon one another and so little about the gifts they hope to receive from each other. Strange, because the whole emphasis in the teaching concerning the functioning of the body (1 Cor. 12) is upon receptiveness. The danger is not that members will say: "You have no need of me" but that they say: "I have no need of you." The danger is not that a church will refuse to pass on to other churches its convictions and insights; the danger is that many churches say, like the church of Laodicea, "I am rich, I have prospered, and I need nothing" (Rev. 3:17). As a matter of fact, every church in the world stands in need of that great enrichment which would come to it if it should open its mind and heart and life for the *charismata*, or gifts of grace which it can receive through the ministry of other churches.

Ecumenical conversation cannot, however, be described only in terms of sharing. It must also be conceived as the attempt to overcome disunity and to arrive at the mutual concord which should characterize the Church of Christ and which is meant to be part of its witness to the world. For a long time the churches which belonged to different confessional families have not been "on speaking terms" with each other. Since the begining of the ecumenical movement the situation has changed. Churches have been drawn out of their isolation and participated in multilateral or bilateral discussions. Theologians, when writing about the theology of other churches, need no longer write out of the imperfect knowledge gathered from books alone, but can do so with that deeper insight which is given by personal encounter.

We have, however, a long way to go before we will be able to say that all churches participating in the ecumenical movement are seriously engaged in the great adventure of truly ecumenical conversation. Too many churches are content to have only friendly co-operative relations with other churches; too often, churches are merely polite to one another when they should be struggling together in order to arrive at a common mind about the content of their witness and the way in which they should express their unity.

What is ecumenical conversation in the light of our common calling on fellowship in Christ? In this matter all of us are still in the learning stage. The following points seem to me to be of special importance:

1) Ecumenical conversation is conversation within the ecumenical circle of which Jesus Christ is the center. We do not come together as people who have to begin by finding a common foundation for their relationships. That foundation has been laid; the starting point is given. We seek koinonia, because there is koinonia in our common submission to Christ, not to an inactive Christ but to the living Christ who gathers His scattered children together.[10] Whatever obstacles we see in front of us, we remain hopeful about the outcome of our encounter because He is at work among us, leading us back to the one fold of which He is the shepherd.

2) Ecumenical conversation is a dialogue the intention of which is to establish true koinonia and which is, therefore, characterized by a readiness to listen, to understand, and so to discover the real convictions of the ecumenical partners.

Martin Buber, who has written deeply penetrating pages on spiritual requirements of meaningful intrahuman conversation, distinguishes between three types of dialogue: the technical dialogue, which seeks only to arrive at practical conclusions and arrangements; the monologue-dressed-up-as-a-dialogue, in which each is really talking to himself and seeks to defeat the others; and the genuine dialogue, which seeks to establish a spiritual relationship be-

10The "basis" of the World Council of Churches can be criticized because of its one-sided emphasis on the divinity of Christ, but this very emphasis has the advantage of bringing out clearly that it is the Christ who is "God and Savior," who creates and renews the koinonia among all those who believe in Him.

tween persons.[11] It can easily happen that what we call ecumenical conversation is in reality only a technical dialogue or a dressed up monologue. But it is clear that our common calling to koinonia obliges us to seek the genuine dialogue.

Such a dialogue has, first of all, a negative function. It must remove the "specters" which stand in the way of real encounter. Buber shows that in personal relationships these specters play a nefarious role. It is the same in the relationships between the churches. Following Buber, we can speak of six such specters[12]: the picture of itself which church A wants to give to church B; the picture of itself which church B wants to give church A; the picture which church A has of church B; the picture which church B has of church A; the picture which church A has of itself; and the picture which church B has of itself. These pictures are amazingly deep-rooted and powerful. During the centuries of isolation they have remained unchallenged. Our churches are not accustomed to see themselves as others see them. Ecumenical conversation must begin with a common attack against all pictures which do not correspond to the basic spiritual realities. Only then is the way open for the real meeting of minds and hearts. Only then can we hope that fellowship will "happen" and that new common insight will be achieved. It is obvious that this requires much time and much patience. It is, therefore, a superficial judgment on the ecumenical movement to say that it spends too much time in talking. As a matter of fact there is not too much, but too little, ecumenical conversation of the kind which creates koinonia.

3) Since the koinonia to which we are called is koinonia in Christ, ecumenical conversation cannot be conceived in terms of negotiation but only in terms of a common struggle to arrive at a common mind about the truth that is in Christ.

We can negotiate about matters which we control ourselves. But when we are concerned with the truth revealed in Christ, negotiation and compromise must be ruled out. Ecumenical conversation is never without the vertical dimension, and that involves respect for truth, not some abstract idea of truth but truth as incarnate in Christ. It is sometimes suggested that the ecumenical

[11]*Die Schriften Über das dialogische Prinzip*, Heidelberg, 1954, p. 152.

[12]Buber, op. cit., p. 265.

movement worships fellowship at the expense of truth, and there is no doubt that this is a real temptation in all ecumenical endeavor. But this cannot happen where the true nature of koinonia is remembered, for koinonia includes necessarily the common recognition that Christ has the first and the last word and that no church, no Christian can be expected to give up what he believes to have received from the Lord.

But if negotiation is ruled out, the common struggle for a common mind is not ruled out. It may become a very real struggle in which there is a clash of convictions. That must be accepted as part of the ecumenical life. The important things are that such a clash does not take the form of a disputation between adversaries but the form of a constructive encounter between partners, and that, however deep the divergence, the struggle for the common mind is not given up as hopeless.

4) Since we are called to koinonia, ecumenical conversation has a value in itself, but in view of our calling to common witness and service, ecumenical conversation should lead to a common proclamation of the gospel and common action in the world.

It is deeply meaningful for churches which have been isolated from each other to discover again that they belong together and to understand each other in a new way. It is, therefore, not necessary that all ecumenical conversations should have immediate results in the form of a specific consensus. But koinonia must at some time find concrete expression in order that witness may be clarified and service may be intensified. That is why ecumenical study is such a vital part of the ecumenical movement. That study is really a systematic attempt to promote ecumenical conversation on subjects which are of vital importance for the faith, life, and work of the churches, and it seeks to arrive at concrete results in the form of an ecumenical consensus which is offered to the churches for their consideration. And there is no doubt that in this way it has helped considerably to widen the area of the common witness and action of the churches.

We must also speak of the relation between the holy communion and the realization of true koinonia between the churches. Here, if anywhere, the paradoxical character of the ecumenical movement is apparent. We seek to give expression to koinonia, but there are as yet insurmountable obstacles to a common celebration of and common participation of all in the very sacrament which represents and establishes koinonia. The basic difficulty is that both those who advocate full intercommunion now and those who are not ready for such intercommunion stand for convictions which the ecumenical movement, by its very nature, must respect. There are really two questions. The first is: What are the implications of the fact that the initiative in the sacramental action is not taken by us, but by Jesus Christ Himself? There are those in many churches who feel strongly that because this is the table of the Lord, no one has the right to exclude anyone who affirms his belief in Jesus Christ. Others, however, are convinced that because the sacrament is instituted by the Lord Himself, there can only be full sacramental fellowship where there is acceptance of what they believe to have been laid down by more than human authority. The first ask: How can anyone be excluded from the Lord's supper whom He has called and whom He has redeemed? The others ask: What right have we to change the nature of the sacrament instituted by Christ Himself through the acceptance of a practice which implies that it is not essential to have it rightly understood or rightly administered?

The second main problem is: What are the implications of the fact that the sacrament is the sacrament of unity? The former take their stand on the conviction that the common participation in the Lord's supper is the natural way to manifest and deepen the koinonia which exists between the churches. The latter believe that full intercommunion must be the expression of such fellowship as is based on agreement in faith and order.[13] Thus each expresses one side of the dialectical nature of the ecumenical movement, for the former seeks to defend the true principle that in the ecumenical movement we have a unity, and the latter defends the equally true principle that that unity is not the full unity which the Church of Christ is meant to have. And each side has an important question to address to the other side. The one question is: Do not your churches by their refusal to admit the members of all other churches in the

[13]A full discussion of the subject would, of course, have to take account of the position of churches which allow "open" communion in the case of meetings for the specific purpose of promoting the reunion of churches.

ecumenical movement to holy communion retard the growth of unity? The other question is: Are the churches which practice open communion among themselves without actually uniting with each other not in danger of showing that "intercommunion apart from the passion for unity merely slackens the tension of desire, and weakens the sense of the seriousness of what is involved in sharing together in the Lord's Supper?"[14]

The first thing that needs to happen in this respect is certainly that each side should take very seriously the question addressed to it. That is the only way to break what seems today an ecumenical deadlock. This unhappy situation which has already caused so much misunderstanding may yet, if we deal with it at a truly spiritual level, prove to be a thorn in the flesh which forces us all to think more deeply about the nature of koinonia as expressed in the sacrament of holy communion. In the meantime a number of churches are pointing the way by quietly and persistently seeking to arrive at specific agreements with other churches on the matter of inter-communion.

Finally, the task of the ecumenical movement is to help the churches realize koinonia in their own midst. For the realization of the wider ecumenical koinonia depends on the presence of real koinonia within the churches themselves. That is the reason why the issues of the relationships between different sectors of the membership of the church have been and are among the main concerns of the ecumenical movement. The co-operation between the clergy and the laity, between men and women, the integration of youth into the life of the Church are ecumenical questions because ecumenism must begin at home, that is, within each congregation, each church. And the underlying question of the transformation of our atomized churches into centers of true koinonia is so vital for the whole life of the Church today that a movement concerned with the common calling of the churches must, on this point especially, help the churches learn from one another and give to one another all they can.

[14]Lesslie Newbigin in *Theology*, June 1958, p. 225.

At the close of this chapter we must briefly indicate how koinonia is related to marturia and to diakonia.

With regard to the first, it is clear that the manifestation of koinonia is part of the witness of the Church. The reason why the churches are to live in fellowship is not only that they will do a more effective job if they corporate. They are to live in fellowship because the lack of fellowship contradicts the gospel of the Lord who died in order to gather into one the scattered children of God. By obeying their common calling to fellowship in Christ the churches remove a true *skandalon* which renders their proclamation inconvincing. They are meant to live in the world as the society which is a true example to other societies. They can do this only by living together as a coherent body.

Diakonia needs to be seen in the light of koinonia because interchurch service, even Christian service, can so easily become a form of philanthropy which thinks in terms of the *needs* of persons, but not in terms of the needs of *persons* who are brethren in Christ. As one church helps another church, it should not only think in terms of the service it can render but also of the koinonia it can help manifest. It happens often that the greatest service which we can render to churches in need is not in the realm of gifts in money or goods, but rather in the realm of active and understanding sympathy. It is diakonia as an expression of koinonia which builds up the body of Christ.

V

THE CALLING TO
UNITY IN CHRIST

---◆---

Now THAT we have explored how unity may grow through the
common response to the common calling we must return to the
question concerning the nature of the unity, the growth of which
we are to expect and to work for. The ecumenical movement is
not concerned with unity in general or unity at any price. There
are many kinds of unity which are not inspired by the Holy Spirit.
The tower of Babel was built by people who were afraid of being
"scattered abroad," but their effort to become "one people" was
not of God, for they wanted to make "a name for themselves"
and it ended in greater division than ever (Gen. 11). We are not
called to gather in our own way and in our own name; we are
called to gather with Christ (Mt. 12:30).

It is, then, essential for the integrity of the ecumenical movement
that we see clearly what unity is to grow up in and through its
life. It must have a common point of orientation in order to have a
common sense of direction. The unity which comes through common witness, common service, or through the establishment of
fellowship is not automatically the true unity which the Church
is meant to have. It could be inspired by the wrong motives or it
could become the meager unity of efficient co-operation. We must,
therefore, ask what the unity is which is worthy of the calling to
which the churches have been called together. Now it is clear

that because of our divisions we cannot at present agree fully on the requirements of full unity in matters of faith and order. But that does not mean that we have nothing to say together on the true nature of Christian unity. In the course of the short history of the ecumenical movement we have already said a number of important things together on that subject.[1] It would seem that, by a common effort to understand together what the New Testament says about the nature of unity in Christ, we may be led to further common affirmations. The following pages represent an attempt to formulate what those affirmations may be.

At this point we turn first to the high priestly prayer of our Lord, contained in the seventeenth chapter of the Gospel of St. John. Precisely because we have heard so very often the words "that they all may be one," we are inclined to take them for granted instead of asking what they mean in the context of the whole prayer.

It is sometimes asked whether there is real justification for using John 17 as the Magna Charta of the ecumenical movement. Must we not look upon the Johannine discourses, including this prayer, as an expression of the personal theology of the author of the gospel rather than a record of words spoken by Jesus Himself? A clear answer to that question has been given by William Temple. He speaks of the Gospel of St. John as a portrait rather than a photograph. The artist does this "by letting his mind and his subject interpenetrate one another and then expressing the result. Each conversation or discourse contained in the Gospel actually took place. But it is so reported as to convey, not only the sounds uttered or the meaning then apprehended, but the meaning which, always there, has been disclosed by life-long meditation." William Temple believes, therefore, that we should read the gospel "in order to enter into the Evangelist's and the Beloved Disciple's communion with the Lord, not asking at each point what was spoken or done, but knowing that as we share the experience, historical and spiritual, from which the Gospel flows we shall come nearer to the heart and mind of Jesus our Lord than ever

[1]See Visser 't Hooft, "Various Meanings of Unity and the Unity which the World Council of Churches Seeks to Promote" in *Ecumenical Review*, October 1955.

our minds could bring us by meditation upon the precise words that He uttered."[2]

What, then, do we learn about unity in John 17? We note, first of all, that the most explicit teaching about unity comes to us in the form of a prayer. That means that the unity to which we are called is unity which is received and not unity which is fabricated by ourselves. The gathering of the scattered children of God is God's own work in which we are allowed to participate and which we cannot possibly take over. And our participation is, in the first place, by opening ourselves up through prayer. Unity is not self-evident. There is no unity in this world that is not constantly threatened. We must pray for the renewal of unity where it exists, for the restoration of unity where it is broken.

Now we should note that the unity here described has different aspects, or dimensions. There is a dimension of height—the vertical dimension which concerns the unity which the Son together with His flock have with the Father. There is a dimension of length—the horizontal dimension in time which concerns the unity of the apostles with those who come later to believe in Jesus. And there is the dimension of breadth—the horizontal dimension in space which has to do with the unity of those in all lands and places who follow the one Lord.

The vertical dimension is the fundamental one and determines and conditions the other dimensions. The high priestly prayer contains three specific references to unity, and each time the same words are used: "That they may be one" or "that they all may be one" (verses 11, 21, and 23). In each of these cases the nature of that unity is described in terms of the perfect unity between the Father and the Son. In verses 11 and 22 the qualifying phrase is "even as we are one" and in verse 21 "even as Thou, Father, art in me, and I in Thee." In other words, the unity for which the Lord prays is, in the very first place, a God-centered unity. Intellectual agreement, readiness to co-operate together, desire for fellowship—these may be good things, but they fall short of the unity for which the Lord prays. That unity is nothing less than a total identification of our wills with the will of God. The unity which we must continue to seek is the unity expressed in the words spoken in the garden: "Not my will but Thine," the unity with God demon-

[2]*Readings in St. John's Gospel*, London, 1939. pp. XVI, XVIII, XIX.

strated in the life and death of the Servant who humbled Himself and became obedient unto death, even death on a cross.

There is also a dimension of length, a horizontal dimension in time. The Lord had at first prayed for the unity of His disciples, those whom the Father had given to Him (verse 9). But from verse 20 onward, His intercession includes "those who are to believe in me through their word," that is, through the apostolic witness. Thus the "all" of the petition "that they may all be one" embraces the generations of the faithful from the beginnings of the Church until the coming of the kingdom. True unity must be unity with those who were entrusted with the original kerygma. However deep and broad our agreement today may be, if it is not rooted in and controlled by the faith once delivered to the saints, it is not the unity for which our Lord prayed.

The third dimension is that of breadth, the horizontal dimension in space. For "all" means also "all" everywhere and from all nations. This unity is world-embracing and seeks to include the scattered children of God in all places. The prologue of the gospel of John had already struck the universal note: "To all who receive Him, who believed in His name, He gave power to become children of God." The theme had been more fully developed in the parable of the good Shepherd. There were to be other sheep which would be brought into the fold under the one Shepherd. These "all" from Jerusalem and Judea and Samaria and from the end of the earth are to find their oneness in their common participation in the divine plan of which Jesus is the center.

But now we come to a paradox. This unity, comparable to the oneness of the Father and the Son, might seem to be a highly esoteric, intangible, mystical unity. What, then, must we make of the fact that, according to Jesus' own words, the purpose and function of this unity is to convince the world that Jesus is truly sent by the Father and that the Father loves and seeks His scattered children everywhere? These words, "so that the world may believe that Thou hast sent me" (verse 23), can only mean that there is something to be seen, that this unity becomes clearly manifest in ways which are sufficiently unusual in the eyes of the world to make people sit up and take notice. If it is to convince them, it must obviously be a unity different from the many unities which they know already—such as social, political, national, cultural, ideological unities. It must be a unity that cannot be explained in terms of the ordinary motives by which men are driven to unity. It must overcome barriers which seem insuperable. It must make man ask: What is this unknown force that brings men together in spite of their separateness? It must refer man back to the One who gathers His people together out of all races and nations. It is, therefore, quite wrong to think of the spiritual unity of John 17 in terms of an invisible unity, as a Platonic idea or a fine sentiment hid in the souls of the faithful, which does not find concrete expression in their common life and their common witness. The world is to believe because of the unity of the church. It is even to know what God has done in Christ because of that unity. That cannot possibly happen if unity remains either an abstract idea or a secret conviction in the hearts of men. The unity that reflects the union of the Father and the Son must become manifest on earth in the actual life of the Church, in its message and in its outward order, in the mutual relations of its members and its united action in the world.

Thus unity is not an aim in itself. Its function is to serve the accomplishment of the divine purpose. This is strongly underlined by the fact that our Lord links the unity of the Church with the glory which He has received from the Father. Note how closely the glory and the unity are related. "The glory which Thou hast given me I have given to them, that they may be one even as we are one" (verse 22). The unity is the manifestation of God's glory incarnate and transmitted by the Son. The *doxa* (glory) is given "in order that" the Church may be one. We would expect to hear that the unity of the Church is necessary to glorify God. We are told, however, that we cannot have unity unless we receive the glory of Christ. Thus once again the emphasis is on God's initiative, and we are warned that disunity amounts to a refusal to accept the gift of the doxa. What does glory mean in this context? How does the receiving of Christ's glory unite the faithful? The glory of Christ is the glory "as of the only Son from the Father" (Jn. 1:14), His participation in the majesty of God. To receive that glory means to be involved in God's work of salvation, to be on His side, to share in His victory over sin and death. This glory unifies because it lifts us above ourselves and sets us in a world of vastly different proportions. Things which seemed important vanish. The one great face of God's victorious love overshadows all. As long as we try to "receive glory from one another and do not seek the glory that comes from the only God" (Jn. 5:44), there can be no unity among us. But those who "hold the faith of our Lord Jesus Christ, the Lord of glory" cannot show partiality (Jas. 2:1). They are one in that their lives are taken up in the divine drama of salvation.

Now this doxa passage also throws light on the relation between the unity and the mission of the Church. In the Old Testament the *kabod Javeh* (glory of God) is the manifestation of God's presence and power in the world. But in the New Testament it is more precisely characterized, especially in 2 Corinthians 3, as the glory inherent in the ministry of reconciliation. Doxa is closely related to the Holy Spirit. A recent study of this relationship[3] comes to the conclusion that the doxa of Christ is the manifestation of the life of the Spirit in the body of Christ as it comes to expression in, and as a result of, the witness to the crucified and risen Lord. If, then, we read that the gift of glory creates the unity of the Church, we must think especially of the total mission of Christ, the salvation which He offers to the world through the cross and the resurrection. Christians become one as they let themselves be used by Him for that great missionary purpose. In other words the great common mission entrusted to the Church creates unity, and that unity itself becomes a powerful missionary force.

For the goal is not the salvation of the faithful apart from the world. Christ has come to save the world (Jn. 12:47). Though at present the world rejects Christ, the great struggle for its salvation continues. The disciples are sent into the world to "testify that the Father has sent His Son as the Savior of the world" (1 Jn. 4:14). Their testimony must be confirmed by the manifestation in their common life of a unity such as cannot be found within the world itself. Thus Christian unity is not a family concern of the Christians; it has cosmic significance and affects the ultimate destiny of the world.

The last reference to unity in the high priestly prayer speaks of the perfection of unity. The Lord prays that His disciples "may be perfected into one," or, as William Temple translates: "They may become full grown into one" (verse 23). Thus we are reminded

[3]Harry R. Boer, *Pentecost and the Missionary Witness of the Church*, Franeker, 1955.

that our search for the true unity must continue until the end of time. Even if all churches in the world would unite today and have a common faith and order, this goal would still be before them. For that ultimate unity in which Christ is all in all is eschatological and belongs in its fullness to the wholly new life of the kingdom. But that does not mean that we have nothing to do but wait for the kingdom. We must believe that even now Christ Himself is at work perfecting the very limited and inadequate unity we have and transforming it into the unity which will express his glory and will convince the world. And this belief will have to find expression in our acts.

In the other classical passage concerning the meaning of unity, the fourth chapter of the epistle to the Ephesians, we find again the three dimensions of unity. The vertical dimension is described as the sharing in the fullness of Christ (verse 13). The horizontal dimension in time finds expression in the affirmation: one body, one faith, one baptism (verses 4, 5). The dimension of breadth, or universality comes out in the "all" of "one God and Father of us all, who is above all and through all and in all" (verse 6).

But Ephesians 4 contains other insights which are of great importance for our understanding of unity. The first is that we must distinguish between the given unity which is inherent in the common calling and the ultimate unity which we should attain. The first verses of the chapter proclaim the unity which consists in the fact that the one God has sent the one Lord to create one body with one faith. That unity exists and continues to exist whether it finds expression in the actual life of the Church or not. We are not asked to create or organize it, but to maintain it. Lack of unity in the churches does not do away with the fundamental fact that God has taken this decisive action and that, in the light of that action, there can be only one Church.

But this given unity demands realization and this realization takes the form of growth, or increase. The unity which the church is meant to have is attained as the church grows "from" Christ "into" Christ, that is, as it lets itself be built by Him and shares increasingly in His fullness. The goal is described in three expressions (verse 13): "The unity of the faith and of the knowledge of the Son of God," "the complete man," and "the measure of the stature of the fullness of Christ." I translate the second of these impressions as "the complete man" because I believe that St. Augustine and Karl Barth are right in their interpretation that this complete man is Christ Himself.[4] St. John used the same word when he spoke of the faithful "being perfected into one" (Jn. 17:23), and the thought of the Church becoming "one new man," that is, of becoming fully and perfectly the body of Christ had already found expression in the Epistle to the Ephesians 2:15. The goal is the oneness of the Church in and with Christ.

Now this passage contains, at the same time, an explicit answer to the question: How does unity grow? It states that unity grows as the gifts of God, which are inherent in the calling, are used for the building up of the body (verses 11-12). Each member of the Church—and, we may add, each part of the Church—has received gifts of grace; these gifts differ; they have to do with the various aspects of the calling of the Church. The gifts are not to be stored away but to serve. The Church is built up in unity when the various specific callings are fulfilled according to their original intention. The unity of the body depends wholly on the harmonious co-operation and mutual service of each part with its specific charisma.

In John 17 it is the gift of glory which is given in order that the Church may be one. In Ephesians 4 it is the gift of grace, expressed in the various specific callings, which builds the Church in its unity. There is no basic difference. In the gift of grace the victorious love of God is manifested. In the gift of glory God's grace is revealed. In both cases unity is achieved as we make a willing, obedient, and grateful response to His design of bringing men together in that unity which exists between the Father and the Son.

What are the conclusions which we should draw from the New Testament teaching about unity for the life of the ecumenical movement?

We must learn to distinguish various meanings, or levels of unity. Much confusion is created by the fact that we use the word "unity" in our ecumenical discussions without defining it sufficiently. We have already distinguished between the unity of the

[4]See *De Civitate Dei* XXII:18, and Barth, *Kirchliche Dogmatik* IV:2:706.

road and the unity of the goal. We must now go further and seek to define four different meanings of unity:

The given unity of the common calling

The growing unity in fulfilling the common calling

The churchly unity in faith and order

The ultimate unity in Christ

Each of these "unities" must be described in relation to the nature and task of the ecumenical movement.

1. *The given unity of the common calling*

This is the point of departure. We could not seek unity if we were not aware that we had all been called by the one God to be members of the one body. That call has found expression once for all in the coming of Jesus Christ and it remains valid whatever the response of men may be. Thus our unity "is not fundamentally in the apprehending or believing, but in the One who is acknowledged," and "it is a unity established and existing in relation to the object of faith and love, the source of forgiveness and new life."[5] The Corinthians may form various parties, but they cannot alter the fact that Christ is not divided and that there is only one Church of God. God does not recognize the existence of parties or separated churches. He continues to deal with His people as one people. As the Faith and Order Conference in Edinburgh (1937) said in its "Affirmation of Unity", "This unity does not consist in the agreement of our minds or the consent of our wills. It is founded in Jesus Christ Himself . . . We are one because we are all the objects of the love and grace of God and called by Him to witness in all the world to His glorious Gospel."

This is the foundation of all Christian unity, the foundation "which is laid, which is Jesus Christ" (1 Cor. 3:10). We know this given unity through our faith in the work of Jesus Christ. We are invited to enter into it. It is not merely our ideal; it is the real and present force of the pressure of our common calling. In this sense it is true that there exists an invisible unity of all who are included in the common calling. But we must add immediately that this invisible unity is meant to become visible.

[5]Claude Welch, *The Reality of the Church*, New York, 1958, pp. 172-73. Welch says that the unity exists "ultimately" not in the apprehending, but it seems to me better to use the word "ultimate" for the final unity which includes the total union of believers with Christ.

2) *The growing unity in fulfilling the common calling*

The call demands response. The foundation is laid in order that a building may be built upon it. The only way to take the given unity of the common calling seriously is to fulfill the calling together. As the members of the Church live the life worthy of the calling, as they render common witness, as they seek to serve each other and meet together the needs of men, as they enter into fellowship with each other, the given unity becomes spiritual reality in their midst. This applies to the common life of the Church where there is no division. The unity in faith and order needs to be constantly undergirded, implemented, and strengthened by the unity of common active obedience to the calling. Unity which does not express itself in, and is not nourished by, marturia, diakonia, and koinonia is sterile unity.

But the same truth is especially relevant for the relationship of churches which are not at one in the realm of doctrine and church order. The only way in which they can express their awareness of the common calling is to go as far as they can go conscientiously in fulfilling their calling together with other churches. As they do so, they discover that, in spite of their discord, a real unity grows up between them. It is often difficult to express that unity in words, for it does not fit in with our traditional theological categories. But the fact of this unity cannot be denied. It manifests itself when churches in the ecumenical movement speak together to the world and act together in the name of Christ. It reveals itself in such common worship and prayer as we have in ecumenical meetings. It must, of course, be realized that this is only the unity of the road, the real but provisional unity characteristic of the situation in which the churches are not fully united, but in which they feel, nevertheless, called to stay together and to live together. And it must, therefore, be made very clear that this relationship is not sufficient. The ecumenical movement becomes unfaithful to its very mission if it begins to consider its own forms of life and the present relationships between the churches as permanent. These structures are to decrease in order that unity may increase. The growth of unity is not to be the growth of a movement or a World Council of Churches, but the growth of the *Una Sancta,* the one Church of Christ.

3) *The churchly unity in faith and order*

Unity in Christ demands visible expression. We have no more right to say that disunity can be overcome by invisible unity, while we continue to live practically in disunity, than to say that we can overcome our sins invisibly, while we continue to commit them. Just as it is erroneous to deny that Jesus Christ came into the flesh, so it is erroneous to deny that the Church is to manifest its unity concretely in tangible forms. We found that the glory of Christ is at stake; the Church is to reveal that glory in its oneness. And we found that the missionary witness of the Church is equally at stake; the unity of the Church is part of its witness to the power and love of its Lord.

Churchly unity means unity in those things which are indispensable for the life of the Church: the common faith, the common sacraments, the common ministry, the common life in each place where the Church is planted. An ecumenical unity which goes together with disagreement in essential questions of doctrine, the impossibility to celebrate and receive the holy communion together, the absence of full recognition of each other's ministry, and the lack of expression of oneness at the level of the local congregation falls short of the unity to which the Church is called.

Churchly unity does not mean centralized unity. The two New Testament passages which we have analyzed say nothing about organizational centralization; their whole emphasis is on unity which grows up in the life of the members themselves. The remarkable thing about the New Testament Church is precisely that it counted wholly on the inherent force of the given unity and of the Holy Spirit to keep the Church united. Similarly churchly unity does not mean uniformity. The New Testament Church is characterized by an almost bewildering variety of ministries and rejoices in the diversity of the gifts of grace.

4) *The ultimate unity in Christ*

The deepest unity is that described in John 17 in the words: "Even as thou, Father, art in me and I in thee" (verse 21, also 22). In Ephesians 4 it is the unity of the "complete man," who is Jesus Christ, and of His fullness (verse 13). We call it the ultimate unity, for, as St. Augustine puts it, growing together in Christ will be "complete in due time."[6] Its full realization belongs to the final consummation.

[6]*De Civitate Dei* XXII:18.

But that it is ultimate does not mean that it belongs merely to the future and that it has no relevance for us today. In both the gospel of St. John and the Epistle to the Ephesians this deepest unity is spoken of as a unity that we may and must seek today. It would be a mistake to think that it will come sometime *after* we have found the unity in the common calling and *after* we have manifested unity in faith and order. On the contrary, it is this unity which determines all other types of unity. This means, more specifically, that we must constantly remember that to share in the common calling and to agree in doctrine and in church order are only means to realize a greater unity, which is purely spiritual in character. "The unity which we must seek is thus a unity which arises from Christ's indwelling in his people, and from their being in him. It is not simply a unity of organization, nor is it simply an agreement about doctrine. It is a total mutual interchange of being—Christ wholly given to us, we wholly given to Him. . . . Its character is most simply described by saying that those participate in it who love one another as Christ loved them."[7]

During our journey on the road we must never lose sight of this goal. For if we strive to receive that unity, all other unities will be added unto us.

[7]Lesslie Newbigin, "The Nature of the Unity We Seek," in *Religion and Life*, Spring 1957.

SUGGESTED PASSAGES FOR BIBLE STUDY
IN CONNECTION WITH
"THE PRESSURE OF OUR
COMMON CALLING"

I *How Does Unity Grow?*
John 17:16–19
Ephesians 4:1–16
Hebrews 3:1–2

II *The Calling to Witness*
Matthew 28:16–20
Acts 1:4–8
Romans 10:9–18

III *The Calling to Service*
2 Corinthians 8:1–15
John 13:1–17
Matthew 25:31–46

IV *The Calling to Fellowship in Christ*
1 John 1:1–17
Philippians 2:1–11
Galatians 2:1–10

V *The Calling to Unity in Christ*
John 17:18–25
Ephesians 4:1–16
1 Corinthians 10:16–18

NOTE: Ephesians 4 is mentioned twice because it is an essential passage concerning calling and growth, as well as one of the essential passages concerning unity.